SELF-DETERMINATION AND HISTORY
IN THE THIRD WORLD

SELF-DETERMINATION
AND HISTORY
IN THE THIRD WORLD

DAVID C. GORDON

PRINCETON UNIVERSITY PRESS
PRINCETON, NEW JERSEY
1971

Library of Congress Catalog card number: 75-141951

ISBN: 0-691-03087-1

Publication of this book has been aided by
the Whitney Darrow Publication Reserve Fund
of Princeton University Press

This book has been composed in Linotype Primer

Printed in the United States of America

by Princeton University Press, Princeton, New Jersey

In Memory of Margaret Foulet
of Cherry Hill Road

CONTENTS

INTRODUCTION

. . . the people are getting ready to begin to go forward again, to put an end to the static period begun by colonization, and to make history.

FRANTZ FANON

The *past*, more or less imaginary or more or less rationalized after the event, acts upon the future with a violence only equaled by the present itself. . . . The real nature of history is to play a part in history itself.

PAUL VALÉRY

"—History," Stephen said, "is a nightmare from which I am trying to awake. . . ."

JAMES JOYCE

INTRODUCTION

HISTORY as the collective memory of a people of its past experiences, its heroes, its great deeds is a basis for its sense of identity, a reservoir upon which it can draw to give itself meaning, and a destiny, as well as to endow its young with a collective pride and dedication to the tribe, the state, the nation, or the religion. This history is an accumulation of myths, illusions, symbols. It is, of course, to be distinguished from the critical, scientific study of history undertaken by scholars for whom the validity of history is determined by objective criteria. Such scholars may, in effect, write from a bias or a viewpoint, conscious or unconscious, but they at least strive for Jacob Burckhardt's "Archimedean point outside events," and seek to describe *wie es eigentlich gewesen*, according to Ranke's aspiration.

The function of the first type of history is utilitarian, to serve the collective interest. The function of the second is to enlighten men in regard to their past experience, without prescribing the use to which this knowledge is to be put. In fact, the two overlap. The Homer of the tribe, and the objective epigone of Ranke, both claim objective validity for what they have to say and, conversely, both are, as men in time and with passions, speaking from a point of view. But the two types of historian are, nevertheless, distinct. To deny this distinction is to

3

deny that the critical scholar is capable of doing more than play tricks upon the dead, as Voltaire once said. It is to deny man's transcendence, his ability to rise above his own collective or the customs of his particular time and place. But to claim for the scholar the possibility of complete objectivity is equally wrong, and were complete objectivity, the holding of a mirror before history, possible, it would tell no more than a mirror does; it would reflect everything and nothing. The scholar producing such work would be an empty abstraction, not a human being. In any case, since R. G. Collingwood and others undermined the articles of faith of the historical positivists, no serious historian, however much he might deny complete relativism, would claim complete scientific objectivity as a possibility for the profession of history.

The value of the first type of history—that of the myth of the collective—is that it makes for unity among those who accept the same myth, inspires people to act in concert, and so multiplies the efficacy of each individual within the group. Conversely, its peril is that it teaches ethnocentricity, keeps alive destructive memories and prejudices, sacrifices reason to emotionalism, and where myths differ and clash, as among the Arabs for example, it can contribute to hinder a people with a common background from realizing a unity which would seem logical and fruitful. One virtue, on the other hand, of scientific history is that it provides a corrective to the first type, but in turn its peril is that it

4

might undermine faith, even produce a spirit of passivity and cynicism, as Nietzsche once warned.[1] The ideal manner of viewing, employing, and teaching one's history might be seen as lying in a tension between the two types of history—history as myth and history as science—the one giving inspiration and a sense of destiny, the other, as a corrective,

[1] *The Use and Abuse of History*, trans. Adrian Collins (Indianapolis/N.Y., 1957). The same point is made by Arthur Schlesinger Jr. in "The Brothers' War" (a review of Thomas J. Pressly, *Americans Interpret Their Civil War*, London, 1954, in *Encounter*, October, 1954, pp. 75-79). Schlesinger argues, among other things, that Herbert Butterfield's distinction between dispassionate "academic" history and melodramatic "contemporary" history is dangerously false; that it leads to a stance that is basically amoral and to a refusal to face evil in an uncertain and tragic world. A different, but not unrelated, danger of "historicism" is the elevation of the "science" of history to an inevitabilitarian cult. It is against this tendency in the post-World War II period that Albert Camus wrote his *L'Homme révolté* (Paris, 1951). The argument of the work is summarized in a statement from Camus' *L'Été* (Paris, 1954) used as an epigraph by Pierre-Henri Simon in *L'Esprit et l'histoire: essai sur la conscience historique dans la littérature du XXᵉ Siècle* (Paris, 1954): "L'Histoire est sans yeux et il faut donc rejeter sa justice pour lui substituer, autant qu'il se peut, celle que l'esprit conçoit." Similarly, one might cite with approval the statement of Alfred von Martin in Hans Kohn, ed., *German History: Some New German Views* (London, 1954), p. 105: "If history is to educate, it must use value judgments in its methodology, that is, it must be considered as the struggle

providing a sense of proportion, a sense of univer-sality. And one possible test of the vitality and the maturity of a people might be considered to be its sense of its own past, and the manner in which it fosters this sense and educates its youth in it to in-clude both an awareness of national specificity and of common humanity with other peoples.

In this present study, under consideration is the conception of history—its uses and abuses, its em-bodiment in myths, its propagation as propaganda and through education—of peoples in the process of self-determination, of revolt against an alien domi-nation—of peoples, in short, in a period of what to-day is fashionably called decolonization. As well as rebelling against an alien imposition that has been political and economic, these peoples, of the newly independent countries of the Third World, are in search of their identity, a search which in the pres-ent context usually means reestablishing links with a past from which they often feel they have been cut off, in several senses, by the colonizing power. They feel the colonizer has disparaged their past in his treatment of their history in order to demoral-ize any possible resistance to the imperial rule; they feel that they have been turned into objects in a historical process whose subjects, whose creative actors, have been the colonizers, not themselves; they seek now both to rewrite their history and also

---

for the realization of values. What must be overcome is the absolutization of the factual, which dates from Hegel."

to enter into history, their own history, as subjects. They wish, in other words, to refashion the continuum from their past to their future, the "creative duration," which, Jacques Berque suggests, "makes us what we are, and increasingly determines what we project."[2] This resurrection of the past is needed because, Muhammed Husayn Haykal, a leading Egyptian intellectual, has said, ". . . a nation whose past is not linked with the present is a creature which neither has a way nor a future,"[3] and Aimé Césaire, the poet, has seen the "intrusion" of colonialism as having rent the vital continuum of African history.[4] Haykal and Césaire are cited here almost at random from among a legion of voices declaring the need for the resumption of this historical continuum, from among contemporary leaders of the movements for decolonization, whether before or after independence.

This emphasis upon history in the struggle for self determination involves history in both of the senses discussed. History as inspiration is to help unite the colonized, to give them a sense of pride

[2] *Dépossession du monde* (Paris, 1964), p. 22. Translations throughout are the author's unless otherwise indicated. Transcriptions of names follow no single system—it is hoped they are clear.

[3] Quoted in Anwar G. Chejne, "The Use of History by Modern Arab Writers," *The Middle East Journal* Autumn, 1960: 382-96.

[4] *Deuxième Congrès des écrivains et artistes noirs* (Rome, 1959), 2 vols., *Présence Africaine*, February-May and August-November (Paris, 1959), I, pp. 116-22.

in the past and so confidence in the future of their people. And history as science is to be rewritten in combat against the pretended scientific history of the colonizer, a history whose ideological bias is to be revealed by the use of the same historical methods the colonizer employs against the colonized. Ultimately the test of whether genuine self-determination, not only political but also cultural and psychic, is being or has been realized is the maturity with which the debate is conducted—and in principle maturity has been attained when the debate becomes obsolete, because those who have once been colonized now have self-confidence in themselves, and are, finally, able to see even in the colonial period of their history, the good as well as the bad— and to perceive in "colonialist" historiography not only what is false, but also what is true.

The focus of this study is principally upon the period following World War I, when peoples either outside the Western World or within but not of the Western World have increasingly rebelled to find political and cultural independence or autonomy. As in Rupert Emerson's *From Empire to Nation*,[5] with whose content the present study overlaps in parts, consideration will be given, for comparative purposes, to a fairly wide range of the experience of decolonization. And unlike many other studies of the use of history for cultural and political purposes, for example Carlton J. Hayes' *France, a Nation of Patriots*,[6] or of historical revisionism, Pieter

[5] Boston, 1960.   [6] New York, 1930.

8

Geyl's *Napoleon, For and Against* and Cyril Black's *Rewriting Russian History*[7] to mention only two, the focus here is upon the non-Western world and upon historical revisionism among peoples whose past is not Western. These peoples are, willy-nilly, forced into a situation in which they feel they must modernize along Western lines and yet at the same time recover a past and a cultural authenticity which is non-Western. It is this last characteristic of the revisionism under discussion which distinguishes it in part, although certainly not completely, from the nationalistic revisionism of a Herder, a Fichte, or the authors of Europe's various *risorgimenti*.

The project here undertaken is of course vast, complex, and often amorphous. Conclusions can only be tentative, but hopefully they will be of interest to those involved in the field of historiography in general, and in the study of decolonization more particularly. The cases studied are limited to those which the author feels he has some competence to handle. They include the cases of the Arab states of the Middle East and North Africa, India and Greece to a limited extent, some African states, Turkey, and the United States with respect to the Black Nationalist movement. Israel is only considered in the context of Arab self-determination.

The author has already touched on the subject

[7] Pieter Geyl, *Napoleon: For and Against* (New Haven, 1949); C. Black, ed., *Rewriting Russian History: Soviet Interpretations of Russia's Past*, 2nd ed. (New York, 1962).

9

of decolonization and history in *The Passing of French Algeria*, and he is grateful to the seminal discussions of the topic by John Wansbrough and Ernest Gellner.[8] The interest and relevance of the topic has been brought home to him from various often disparate sources. Among these are James Joyce's treatment of the nightmare of Irish history in *Ulysses*, the works of Valéry and Fanon,[9] from which citations appear as epigraphs to the present Introduction, and Jacques Berque's sparkling, poetic booklet entitled *Dépossession du monde*.

The author is also grateful to Leon Carl Brown for helpful comments made orally or in written but hitherto unpublished form, and to Charles Gallagher for pointed remarks made during a seminar in which a draft of Chapter Three was discussed. Neither is responsible, of course, for the possible naïveté of the author's diagnoses and prescriptions. The author, finally, owes a debt to Roger Paret for

[8] *The Passing of French Algeria* (London, 1966), pp. 183-90; Ernest Gellner, "The Struggle for Morocco's Past," *The Middle East Journal* Winter, 1961: 79-90; John Wansbrough, "The Decolonization of North African History," *Journal of African History* ix: 4 (1968): 643-50. Among many fascinating cases not treated in the present volume is what one scholar describes as the first case of the reaction of "subject peoples against imperialist historiography," that of the subject peoples of imperial Russia. See *The Times Literary Supplement*, August 8, 1968: 853.

[9] Frantz Fanon, *The Wretched of the Earth*, trans. Constance Farrington (New York, 1968), p. 54. Paul Valéry, *Reflections on the World Today*, trans. Francis Scarfe (New York, 1958), p. 12.

10

his brilliant essay-review of Charles André Julien's most recent work, in which Paret concludes: "The liberty of a people is its right to history, but history like liberty only belongs to those who have conquered it."[10]

[10] "Quand l'Algérie ne savait pas qu'elle était algérienne . . . ," *Preuves* October, 1966: 68-79. Julien's book reviewed is *Histoire de l'Algérie contemporaine*, vol. I: *La conquête et les débuts de la colonisation (1827-1871)* (Paris, 1964). The present author would also like to thank the following for their assistance: Dr. Constantine Zurayk, R. M. Ardill, Sandra Killon, and, especially, Reader "A."

1

THE QUEST FOR HISTORY

WHATEVER the "structuralists" like Lévi-Strauss, the behavioral psychologists such as B. F. Skinner, or the successful managerial futurists like Henry Ford, Sr., might say, to the leaders of national liberation movements or to the leaders of developing nations, history is not "bunk." On the contrary, history to these leaders is of the essence. This concern, if not obsession, with the past of one's own people takes many shapes, sometimes contradictory, usually passionate: it ranges from the feeling that history is a nightmare from which one must awake, a history that must be exorcised, to the feeling that an illustrious past that the colonialist has disparaged must be resurrected.

The importance of history among those engaged in the struggle for independence has been most explicitly expressed, perhaps, in the writing of two leading students and ideologues of decolonization, Albert Memmi, a Tunisian Jew by origin,[1] and Frantz Fanon, now something of a prophet to groups as far-ranging as the Black Nationalists of the United States, the Palestinian *Fidayeen*, and the revolutionaries of the Algerian Revolution. Each of these two writers apparently arrived independently at quite similar conclusions about the nature of the colonial situation, the need for revolution, and the important role of history in this struggle. And both,

[1] Since 1960, Memmi has taught social psychiatry at the École Pratique des Hautes Études (the Sorbonne).

15

symbolically, had their two most seminal books introduced by Jean-Paul Sartre, the grand old man of the revolutionary rejection of Western domination.[2] Memmi in his typical, succinct, epigrammatic manner states unequivocally:

> The most serious blow suffered by the colonized is being removed from history and from the community. Colonization usurps from him any free role in either war or peace, every decision contributing to his destiny and that of the world, and all cultural and social responsibility. . . . He is in no way a subject of history any more. . . . He has forgotten how to participate actively in history and no longer even asks to do so.[3]

The colonized becomes a petrified object in his own country; the history he is taught is that of the colonizer, and his streets and squares are bedecked with the heroes and symbols of the colonizer. It is not strange, therefore, that when he finally decides to resist, the colonized will look for sources of strength and encouragement in his past.[4] He will

[2] Memmi, trans. Howard Greenfeld, *The Colonizer and the Colonized* (N.Y., 1965) and Fanon, *The Wretched of the Earth.*

[3] pp. 91-92.

[4] In regard to the case of Palestine, Pierre Vidal-Naquet, in a review of a number of anti-Zionist books, echoes Memmi when he writes that the Palestinians now wish to apply to themselves the formula once applied to the Jews, they wish to become "subjects" in history (*Le Monde*, July 30, 1969). Karl W. Deutsch in *Nationalism and Social Communication: An Inquiry into the Foundations of Nationality* (New Haven, 1953), p. 139, describes the term

resurrect or create myths of his own to counteract the myths of the colonizer. Thus, to cite an extreme case, a Malcolm X will see the first men as black (as God Himself), and he will, mythically, identify his people with the history of Islam to combat Christianity, the religion of the whites.[5] Memmi does not condone the abuse of scientific history that this often involves; he simply sees it as an inevitable, although negative, moment in the process of self-determination.[6]

Frantz Fanon has much the same to say, but he is more apocalyptic and more optimistic as to the possibility of a "new man" emerging through the violent repudiation of Western domination and Western culture.[7] He can write, for example, "It is a question of the Third World starting a new history of Man."[8] Like Memmi, however, Fanon sees the

---

"awakening," so often applied to the rise of nationalism among Western and non-Western peoples alike, as meaning an attempt to recover the energy and the vision of a period in past history.

[5] Memmi, *L'Homme dominé: essais* (Paris, 1968), pp. 20-21.

[6] It might be observed that among non-historians who have sought to evoke the history of their people are fictional writers like Albert Memmi himself, in several novels, and, most talented of all the North African creative writers, Kateb Yacine. See the author's *North Africa's French Legacy* (Cambridge, Mass., 1962), ch. 6.

[7] On Fanon, see the present author's essay in *The Passing of French Algeria*, pp. 121-32.

[8] p. 254. Fanon's peculiar emphasis on violence may, ironically, only deepen the sickness he seeks to remedy. This is not so of Memmi. In the framework of the triple

colonized living in "an unchanging dream," while the colonizer makes history. It is only with the revolution of decolonization that the colonized reenters history, begins "to make history." It is through the struggle itself that he realizes his community with his fellows, gains with them a sense of a "national destiny." He cultivates the heroes of his own past, Samory, Abdelkader, and many others. On the other hand, and again as for Memmi, for Fanon the exploitation by the colonized of his past, his cultivation of his uniqueness mythically, is only a moment, historically, in his access to universality. Thus the cult of an African Negro past, for example, gives way to the moment of immediate national consciousness; the cultivation of "national culture" which is the product of a general revolution, almost inevitably violent for Fanon, is ultimately a stage toward genuine universality, a dialogue among free people. Thus Memmi and Fanon, while they deeply sense the importance of the historical recreation of the past as a stage in revolution, and while both insist that the colonized must recapture the feeling that he is a participant, a creative factor in history, they see historical self-determination as ultimately a way to attain to the universal, the human generally.

---

classification of historical perspectives adopted below, Fanon would be best classified as a "futurist" and with regard to his more chiliastic pronouncements, one might venture to refer to him as an "eschatological" futurist, that is, a person who believes in the possibility of a dramatic leap into an almost predestined and qualitatively new future.

18

But being intellectuals involved in the active political struggle for self-determination, they inevitably emphasized negativity, even while recognizing such negativity as pathological. Thus, Fanon is partly autobiographical when he talks of the unrooted, foreign-educated, colonized intellectual whose quest for a "national culture" derives from the psychological need to find an "anchorage" among his people, a people from whom colonialism has cut him off, and who becomes obsessively absorbed with the "unique" historical destiny of this people.[9]

Among similar cases, among intellectuals and leaders of the Third World, of self-consciousness about history and of the impulse to recover the past is that of Algeria's present Minister of Education, Ahmed Taleb, who, as son of Sheikh al-Ibrahimi, leader of the Association of the Reformist 'Ulema, and as a French educated medical doctor, bridges Algeria's two legacies, the French and the Islamic. To him, while it is essential that Algeria modernize, the past, preserved thinly during the colonial period in folk poetry and in the Koranic schools of his father's Association, must be revived, and Arabic must become the national language as rapidly as is possible.[10] He also, like Memmi and Fanon, sees the

[9] p. 175.
[10] "La Décolonisation culturelle en Algérie," *Jeune Afrique* December 10-16, 1962: 26-27. Malek Bennabi, *Vocation de l'Islam* (Paris, 1954), pp. 99-101, says much the same. Following a description of the withering of Algerian customs and institutions under colonial rule, he writes: "The colonial act is an immense sabotage of history."

19

national culture as having been "mummified" under French rule, as needing to be revivified (through the reacquisition of Arabic as a language of culture), so that the Algerian might define his future "by his history." While Taleb is in favor of retaining the best of the colonial heritage, he is also in favor of shedding the "*séquelles impalpables*" of the French cultural overlay. Only by returning to its own historical culture can Algeria borrow creatively and fruitfully, rather than imitatively and destructively.

Taleb's theme, however, raises the question—one to be explored later—whether the past he speaks of can, first, be resurrected in the modern world, and, second, whether the French "overlay" may not be, for good or bad, an intrinsic part of modern Algeria. Taleb's argument is typical of many intellectuals of new nations who are more often inspired by sensibility than by historical realism.

But to turn from Algeria to quite a different context, that of the United States, Herbert Aptheker, speaking for the American Negro, reveals the same concern for history as do Fanon, Memmi, and Taleb when he says: "History's potency is mighty. The oppressed need it for identity and inspiration; oppressors for justification, rationalization, and legitimacy. Nothing illustrates this more clearly than the history writing on the American Negro people."[11] And

[11] Quoted in John H. Clarke, *William Styron's Nat Turner: Ten Black Writers Respond* (Boston, 1968), p. vii. Aptheker, a white Marxist, would presumably consider the historiographical agitation of blacks in America only a dialectical moment in a historical sequence leading to a

20

E. U. Essien-Udom, in his *Black Nationalist: A Search for an Identity in America*, observes that the extravagant "eschatology" of the Black Moslems "expresses the nationalist's need to attach himself in a positive way to something worthy and esteemed, some center of power, some tradition, and, generally, some 'central ideal' capable of endowing his life with meaning and purpose."[12]

Another example of the historical impulse among American Blacks is that of Nathan Hare, of San Francisco State, who described the new Department of Black Studies, of which he was director, as "designed to regenerate the mortified ego of the black

raceless as well as classless society. Staughton Lynd, in "Historical Past and Existential Present," in Theodore Roszak, ed., *The Dissenting Academy* (London, 1968), pp. 87-101, p. 90, says of his experience teaching at a Negro women's college in Atlanta: "For my Negro students it was almost as important to know the true character of their collective past as to be at case with their personal histories."

[12] Chicago, 1962, p. 123. Note that Essien-Udom, appropriately, uses the religious term "eschatology," rather than "myth," for the continuum that a people whose separation from their historical past is so extreme seek to establish. In the present study, it might be made clear, the term "myth" is not used pejoratively as equivalent to falsehood. It rather refers to an imaginative reconstruction of the past that raises this past to an epic level, blending fact and fiction in various proportions. An excellent discussion of the nature and role of "myth," in the context of the historiography of the French Revolution, appears in R. R. Palmer, *1789: les révolutions de la liberté et de l'égalité* (Paris, 1968), ch. x.

child. A proud black history can restore and construct a sense of pastness, of collective destiny, as a springboard to the quest for a new collective future."[13] At Princeton University a young black student said of newly introduced courses on negro history and culture: "It's ammunition. . . . Lots of white people have no appreciation of what black people have achieved. So it's good for us to know about our history and our writers."[14] And another said: "And it's psychologically nourishing. . . . Many of us grew up with the feeling that Negroes as a whole aren't good for much. This kind of course helps us get over that. And we won't pass the 'no good' ideas on to our kids; we'll know they just aren't so." Finally, in regard to the American black's thirst for history, the answer to an article by Joseph Alsop disparaging Black Studies programs might be cited. The writer, Claude Singer, makes a point that, sadly, is difficult to gainsay: "If, having been deprived of a cultural heritage and the symbols of racial pride, black Americans find in history that which they specifically look for. I think they are eminently justified. At the very least, they would be no different from conventional American historians who have for decades fashioned elaborate myths in the name of historical truth."[15]

[13] *Encounter* May, 1969: 37.

[14] "A Black Seminar: The Search for Identity," *Princeton Alumni Weekly* March 4, 1969: 8-9.

[15] *The International Herald Tribune* February 22-23, 1969.

The resort to history can also be used for polemical purposes, to meet the pretensions of a colonialist enemy in debate, as well as to discover the cause of the predicament of one's own people. A case in point is Dr. Anthony Zahlan, chairman of the Physics Department of the American University of Beirut, who has turned himself into something of a sociologist-historian in the struggle for Palestinian liberation from Zionist Israel. Representative of many articles he has written is one entitled "Support for Israel: A Legacy" in which he seeks to discover the historical reasons for what, to him, is the United States' obsessive support of the Zionist cause.[16] Zahlan thus becomes something of an ally of Constantine Zurayk, Professor of History at the same university and a lifelong intellectual leader of the Arab cause, who in many articles and books has sought to reanimate the Arab world by attempting to make it historically conscious and so honest enough with itself to see its weaknesses, as well as to draw inspiration from its past strength.[17]

Another Third World intellectual to make a polemical use of history was Mehdi Ben Barka, the late

[16] *The Middle East News Letter* (Beirut) January-February, 1969: 11-16.

[17] See *Nahnu wa al-Tarikh*, 2nd ed. (Beirut, 1963). To an extent, Zurayk and his late colleague Professor Nabih Faris, both of the History Department of the American University of Beirut, sacrificed something of their professional careers in order to serve the Arab cause actively, a sad but understandable sacrifice professional history must make to engagement during any struggle for self-determination.

23

leader of the Moroccan Left. On the surface, it is strange to find a man whom Abdallah Laroui has correctly described[18] as a *technophile*, that is, a person who sees his people as backward, ignores the specificity of their culture, and seeks progress purely in terms of science, being concerned with the history of his people. But Ben Barka was, in fact, a close student of Moroccan history and studied it in order to find, among other things, arguments against the theses of the French protectorate and, after independence, against the presumption of the King to rule absolutely.[19] Even if not concerned particularly with the specificity of his people, he sought in history a weapon in their behalf out of devotion to them. On the importance of history in the context of decolonization he has added an aggressive note, to wit, that now the East will turn upon the West historiographically:

> When a people begins to talk about itself and its past, it has become adult. During the last centuries it has been the Europeans who have written and discoursed about us, as they have written about India and China, and for some of them, this was the mark itself of Western superiority. Today, we begin again to speak about the West

[18] *L'Idéologie arabe contemporaine* (Paris, 1967), pp. 25 ff.

[19] See Abdelkader Ben Barka, *El Mehdi Ben Barka mon frère* (Paris, 1966), p. 74. And see Mehdi Ben Barka's introduction to Mohammed Lahbabi's *Le Gouvernement marocain à l'aube du XXᵉ siècle* (Rabat, 1958).

24

and to judge its actions. Historical equality is thus reestablished.[20]

Ben Barka's aggressive threat to turn historiography against the colonizers of the West would seem, in part, to be impelled by a desire to take revenge for the way the West has heretofore interpreted the East. One might hope that his impulse was also to seek enlightenment. In any case, it illustrates the resentment of the colonized at the way the colonizer has dominated the writing and the interpretation of the history of the colonized peoples. A characteristic expression of this resentment appears in Abdelkader Ben Barka's tribute to his brother Mehdi, after the latter's disappearance and probable murder. He is cited here because he is representative of many educated North Africans who are neither historians nor particularly outstanding minds.

While at school, Abdelkader Ben Barka states, he and his companions deeply resented the fact that the history they were regaled with was nearly exclusively that of France, to the almost complete neglect of North African history. In reaction against such cultural colonialism, Ben Barka and his friends not only turned French history against France by referring to the ideals of the French Revolution, but they also began to cultivate the study of their own history, to discover, for example, that La Fontaine's tales had already been told in *Khalila wa dimna*; that Pope Sylvester II (Gerbert) had to study at

[20] Introduction to Lahbabi, *op. cit.*, p. 3.

Muslim universities to be able to introduce Arabic numerals into Europe; that while Europe was in a state of relative ignorance, North Africa produced geniuses like Averroes, Idrissi, the geographer, and Ibn Khaldun.[21] It was with this pride that these *évolués* shocked their French colleagues by throwing ashes on their heads and chanting the traditional prayer, the *latif*, as a declaration of their historical independence, of their repudiation of French cultural despotism.[22] But while one can sympathize with the desire of Ben Barka for cultural independence, his position raises the question as to how useful it is to rationalize present weakness by the evocation of past dynamism and glory, and whether the attitude that it implies represents genuine psychic emancipation.

On a more sophisticated level, Abdallah Laroui takes Western historians and Orientalists to task for judging Islamic history according to Western standards (as the norm). He is particularly critical of "Anglo-Saxon" historians who, influenced by their Protestant and/or liberal Western commitments, disparage the Arabs for being apparently unable to sustain Western institutions (parliamentary government, for one), and who seek (W. C. Smith, for

[21] Needless to say, such claims by Arab nationalists for their past may be exaggerated or debatable in detail, but in general they are perfectly valid. Salah-Eddine Tlatli defends Tunisia's pre-colonial past in much the same way as does Abdelkader Ben Barka in *Tunisie nouvelle: problèmes et perspectives* (Tunis, 1957), pp. 218-21.

[22] Abdelkader Ben Barka, *op. cit.*, pp. 55-57.

26

example) implicitly to encourage Muslims to shed their traditions and, in effect, become Protestants.[23] And on a less sophisticated level, the Senegalese intellectual Cheikh Anta Diop can accuse Western ers of having destroyed countless Egyptian mummies that provided the historical evidence that the Egyptians "who civilized the world" were in effect African Negroes.[24] This reaction against the Western treatment of the history of the colonized, or once colonized, will be more fully considered in Chapter Three. It is introduced here only to illustrate the polemical impulse of those seeking self-determination, who, stimulated by resentment against the historiography of the colonizer, seek "ammunition" in history.

While these various persons cited all have in common a concern with history, their attitudes toward the role of their past in the contemporary struggle for self-determination vary. Three approaches evident among them—never completely distinct in reality, of course, and rather tendencies than defined attitudes—are suggested for purposes of analysis: the "futurist" whose proponents feel history must be exorcised and transcended, the "apologist" whose advocates believe that salvation and power in the present can be found through a return to a specific past tradition, and the "resurrectionalist" whose proponents feel a progressive future can only be based upon a reinvigorated past.

[23] Laroui, *op. cit.* Wilfred C. Smith's work referred to is *Islam in Modern History* (Princeton, 1957).

[24] *Nations nègres et culture* (Paris, 1955), p. 19.

All three approaches have in common a concern with history, positive or negative, and the conviction that during the colonial period the colonized people have been in one sense or another excluded from history, have been denied a creative role on the world's historical stage. All three seek to come to terms with the past in order to enter more effectively into possession of the techniques and principles by which the West has been able in the recent past, or is currently able, to dominate them. This impulse Berque has neatly characterized as the quest to combine "authenticity with efficacy," that is, to enter the modern industrial and scientific world, but to do so in terms of one's historical personality through a return to one's own historical continuum, interrupted by the colonialist period.[25] It might be ob-

[25] Berque, op. cit., p. 136. After conducting an extensive number of interviews for the author (in 1969) with Tunisian history teachers and historians, Rashad al-Imam, candidate for the Ph.D. at the American University of Beirut, came to the conclusion, quite independently of the author, that these men involved in history could be ideologically divided into three groups, each one of which corresponds to one or another of the three groups described in the present study. The first group al-Imam designated as those who have no use for Tunisia's traditional heritage, religious or otherwise, and seek to transform Tunisia into a progressive socialist state on the basis of "science." Generally, members of this group, that is the "futurists," were educated in France. Members of the second group, usually products of traditionalist education in Arabic at the Zaitouni University, are "apologists" and hostile to Westernization. And the third group, mostly products of a mixed French and Arabic education (at the Collège Sadiqi in particular), seek a

jected that the futurist described does not fit into this general pattern, but as will be argued in what follows, he too, in effect, thinks in terms of his people's "personality," if only by implication, and he certainly thinks that his people must, as they once did in however primitive conditions, play a role in history as subjects and no longer objects manipulated by people of another culture, another history.

THE PERSPECTIVE OF THE FUTURIST

Of Mehdi Ben Barka, considered a model of the futurist, it has already been indicated that while history to him was a weapon to free his people, he had no particular interest in the historical specificity of his people, or in resurrecting a past tradition best left dead. It might be used, indeed, interpretatively, as a basis for combating the colonizer and then for improving the present along democratic lines—a use Ben Barka did in fact make of it—but basically, as Laroui has observed, Ben Barka thought in terms of a brave future molded according to the scientific principles of world socialism, not in terms of a great and glorious past.

A similar spirit permeates the work of the Moroccan playwright Muhammad Ben Shakrun, whose Arabic Theater Troupe (of Rabat) traveled throughout Morocco presenting his satiric plays. He has been called the Molière of Morocco and, to his amusement, he was highly praised by the French

---

balance between the Western and the traditional—they are, in short, "reconstructionalists."

because of the fun that he made of old and traditional Moroccan ways. But to believe Ben Shakrun himself, his intent was polemically anti-French. "The Moroccans," he once told an interviewer,

... must be awakened from their oriental routine, if not they will remain a colonial people. Not in vain do the French support the old, corrupt, feudal institutions of Morocco, because in the circles of the Pashas and Caids they find people who in a free, modern Morocco would fear for their power and position and so degrade themselves as handymen of the French oppressor. When in my theater pieces I caricature the old regime, and make inherited traditions laughable, at the same time I strike a blow at the colonialist system.[26]

The colonialist system once shed, the weapon of social satire will presumably be used to help clear the relics of the past from the path of a progressive future, and so, one would assume, challenge oppression that might come from native sources.

A final Moroccan to be discussed in the present context is Abdallah Laroui, already cited as a critic of Mehdi Ben Barka's indifference to Morocco's cultural specificity.[27] Laroui's views are difficult to grasp easily, but although he seems to argue that the future can only be built upon an awareness of the national state's cultural heritage, there are ele-

[26] Herbert Reichard, *Westlich von Mohammed: Geschick und Geschichte der Berber* (Cologne, Berlin, 1957), p. 95.
[27] Laroui, *op. cit.*

ments in his "ideology" which militate against the cult of the past, against any resurrection of the past which would prove retrogressive. Thus, while he warns against the "intellectual terrorism" of the "*technophiles*," like Ben Barka, he also repudiates the apologetic approach of the "clerks," the Muslim elders, who by arguing that liberal principles are inherent in Islam refuse to be critical of the contemporary Islamic reality. And Laroui is also critical of the "politicians" who, won over to Western liberal principles, pridefully and naïvely interpret their history to discover these liberal principles already present in their heritage. To both clerks and politicians the Arabic language and the great historical past become a fetish, a "*mythe protecteur*," which makes for a false sense of identity and a false sense of comfort. Thus, for example, the exoticist cultivation of the past by the Arab bourgeois, his interest in folklore, in archaic art forms and the like, is not a return to authenticity, but rather an imitation of the Westerner's new-found taste for a colorful past which is dead and gone. The Arab bourgeois plays the Westerner's game. To the traditionalist, of course, Laroui is also playing the "West's game," and, to the liberal "politicians," he is undermining his people's confidence that in modernizing they are in part developing elements of their own proper tradition. But Laroui's futurism, as seen, is tempered by a recognition of the importance of the historical tradition of a people as a factor in modernization, even if he does seem at times to be trying to square the circle. Further, it is to his credit that he insists

31

upon historical objectivity as the inevitable price of integrity and therefore genuine independence, that he condemns unequivocally the use of history as a tactic of evasion.

In the context of Algeria, Abdallah Mazouni has undertaken a similar attack on the evasive apologetic nature of much contemporary Arab historiography.[28] Focusing on very recent history—that of the background and course of the Algerian Revolution—he takes to task those apologists who, since independence, have sought to defend the *status quo* by asserting that the Revolution was essentially a struggle to resurrect an Islamic-Arabic past. Such apologists obfuscate the fact that most of the leaders who launched the Revolution in 1954 were "modern nationalists" with socialist orientations and proletarian backgrounds, and that many people came to support the Revolution for purely secular reasons. Mazouni insists, therefore, that it is unhistorical as well as unjust to exclude any revolutionary from the pantheon of independent Algeria's architects because of any alleged lack of Arab-Muslim "purity." More broadly, he insists that the Revolution was not only a rejection of colonial rule: it was also a rebellion against all those elements in Algerian heritage which make Algeria a backward country. Genuine *"répersonalisation"* means coming to terms with the modern world and with socialism as well as with the past. As well as rejecting any narrow, purely Arab-Muslim conception of Algeria's Revolution, Mazouni

[28] *Culture et enseignement en Algerie et en Maghreb* (Paris, 1969), pp. 27, 59, 78, 97-112, in particular.

32

also considers that it is absurd to pervert earlier history for purposes of self-esteem. Thus he suggests that it is foolish to claim St. Augustine as part of Algeria's heritage simply because he, in particular, happened to have been a Berber. St. Augustine belongs to a different tradition—the Western Christian—and not to the Algerian; although, he observes, St. Augustine, like all other great cultural leaders, of course, belongs to universal culture as such. In any case, Mazouni concludes, the worship of that past by some contemporary Algerian apologists is a pathological escape from the real issues of the present.

The Arab world in general has, of course, a very rich cultural heritage and it knew an efficacy in the past which the world in general appreciates and honors today. But what of peoples whose past is little known, little respected, much less compatible with modernization than is the case with the Arabs or the Indians or the Chinese? Might not the temptation to futurism be overwhelming? Might not the past be simply a nightmare to awaken from? The part of the world where this is most true today, in the eyes of both outsiders and in the eyes of many of its inhabitants, is sub-Sahara Africa.[29]

The anguish induced by the concern over the historical past and its relation to the construction of a new African nation was poignantly expressed by Dr.

[29] Emerson, *op. cit.*, p. 152, points up the irony of Africans, particularly the urbanized, wishing to return to a past whose tribalism could only be disruptive to the national unity they wish to realize.

Kenneth Onwuka Dike, the Principal of University College, Ibadan, in 1957:

If the African has no past heritage, and no future except by imitation of European ways at a pace which the European thinks safe, then the Gold Coast is destined to fail. But if the instinctive belief of the African in his tradition is justified, the ultimate emergence of West African states as independent states cannot be doubted. . . . Every nation builds its future on its past; so the African must not only instinctively have faith in his own existence, but must also satisfy himself by scientific inquiry that it exists.[30]

While asserting the existence of a heritage upon which to build, Dike reveals a lack of assurance when he says this heritage, so insecurely known or possessed, must be sought for and scientifically ascertained. Dike, of course, is not a futurist; he seeks to overcome his unease in regard to the African past

[30] Quoted in Emerson, *op. cit.*, p. 154. In another part of this speech, as quoted by Charles J. Patterson in "CJP-10 The First International Congress of Africanists," December 18, 1962, Institute of Current World Affairs, p. 7, Dike said: "Our newly acquired independence must be without meaning if it implies mere imitation of Western ways. Africa like every other continent in history must build on its past . . . for it is no use inventing a romantic past which has no relation to reality; we must accept that our past like the past of the rest of the world has its good and bad aspects. We must accept the glories of Benin art with the human sacrifices, just as the Spaniard accepts the horrors and bigotries of the Inquisition with the achievements of El Greco and Cervantes."

34

through historical exploration. But this same unease often suggests to other African intellectuals the opposite approach, that of transcending a vaguely known or unwanted past through its rejection and through a dedication to a "modern" future. In general, futurist intellectuals are more likely to be found among Africans born and educated in the British rather than the French context, and they tend, often, to belittle the pretensions of the French-educated advocates of *Négritude* as romantics and even reactionaries.[31] Such a futurist was Ndabaningi Sithole.[32] While denouncing the evils of colonialism, he does give colonialism credit for suppressing slavery and the slave trade, and for ending a situation in which "the chief occupation of most able-bodied African men was that of raiding other tribes." Tribalism, he states, has been undermined through improved communications and the rise of industrial cities where members of different tribes have melted

[31] An attack on futurism by a leader of *Négritude* was made by Aimé Césaire at the First International Conference of African Writers, held in Paris in 1956. He warned against the temptation of a *tabula rasa*. Cited in Hans Kohn and Wallace Sokolsky, *African Nationalism in the Twentieth Century* (Princeton, 1965), p. 151.

[32] *African Nationalism* (Cape Town, 1959). Kohn and Sokolsky, *op. cit.*, pp. 73-74, observe that in statements made elsewhere, Sithole seems to have contradicted the "futurism" of his attitude in this book. He has defended the "African personality" concept as a barrier to total Europeanization, as the expression of a desire of Africans to remain true to their destiny. In respect to such statements, Sithole reveals his "apologetic" side.

35

into a common people, transcending their tribalism. "The twentieth-century African nationalism," he writes, "is indeed the child of European colonialism."[33]

Apparently accepting the "idea of progress"—the notion that human progress is universal and mono-linear in time and that civilization is one, not multiple—Sithole states that because of modern technology Africa need not repeat Europe's two-thousand-year history, but in spite of the "absence of an imposing black civilization" enter at once into the struggle to "civilize the African."[34]

It is this futurist attitude which a number of Kenyan students at the American University of Beirut have revealed to the present author when they express doubt about the value of resurrecting a past that is tribalist and which might only serve to rekindle the animosities best buried.[35] While showing

[33] Sithole, op. cit., p. 74.

[34] Ibid., p. 163. Sithole here echoes Comte's thesis that men are all alike basically, and that diversity will disappear as the rest of the world adopts, ineluctably, the model of Western industrial society. On Comte's unilinear view of human history see Raymond Aron, Les Étapes de la pensée sociologique (Paris, 1967), pp. 86-87.

[35] Elspeth Huxley, in a very pessimistic, almost cynical, account of African development, sees Kenyatta's Facing Mount Kenya (1938) as a dangerous defense of Africa's past, openly defending the values of tribalism. See "What Future for Africa? II," Encounter June, 1961: 8-20. President Kenyatta, of course, wrote his book during the negative historical moment of revolt. Today, against great odds, he seeks to promote national as opposed to tribalistic values. But the threat of tribalism to Kenyan unity remains

36

a great interest in Western history, they expressed wariness at encouraging the study of their own past among the young of Kenya. But as Sithole reacts defensively[36] when African "primitivism" is pressed in Western books, so these Kenyan students have an obvious love for many aspects of their heritage, of their music in particular, and they resent any disparagement of their culture by outsiders. The statements of futurists, in short, should not always be taken at their face value, anymore than some of the statements made by apologists.

Another qualification to the categories used in this chapter is that the distinction between apologist and futurist is often only a question of temperament, and of opinion as to the nature and the possibilities of historical change, not of a difference over the desirability of a progressive future. A case in point was a prototypical debate on the shores of Lake Como in 1963 when Khodadad Farmanfarmaian, Deputy Governor of the Central Bank of Iran, a futurist in this context, and Professor Yusuf Ibish, of the American University of Beirut, an ideologically committed orthodox Muslim, but also a modernizer, clashed over the issue of change in the Muslim

---

dangerous, as became apparent following the assassination of Tom Mboya in 1969 and the currency of rumors that Kenyatta himself had participated in ritual oaths taken by Kikuyus to keep themselves in power even by violence if necessary. See R. W. Apple Jr., "Cracks in Kenyan Unity," *The International Herald Tribune* October 16, 1969.

[36] *Op. cit.*, pp. 100 ff.

world.[37] Farmanfarmaian argued that no matter what "images" were shattered, economic development must be pushed at all costs in an underdeveloped country. Other social institutions would have to adjust to the change as best they could. Ibish, on the other hand, argued that change which did not take account of deep-rooted traditions, religion or the extended family, for example, would produce chaos, would awaken the "sleeping giant" of anarchic mass movements. It is this danger of leaping into an unknown future while abandoning a traditional present in which the individual at least has some roots, some sense of belonging, that partly justifies the stance of the apologist at his best and, conversely, makes the futurist, at his most extreme, suspect.[38]

THE PERSPECTIVE OF THE APOLOGIST

The apologist's contribution, then, is to question the propriety and the realism of making short

[37] K. N. Silvert, ed., *Discussion at Bellagio: the Political Alternatives of Development* (New York, 1964), pp. 50-60.

[38] A suggestive corrective to the facile optimism of some futurists is Herbert Lüthy, "L'Europe reste à décoloniser," *Preuves* May-June, 1969: 8-12. Remarking on recent expressions of regional nationalism (among the Welsh, the Bretons, the Flemish, and the Tyrolese), he states, half-sardonically, half-seriously: "The futurists [*futurologues*] are persistently wrong in seeking the future anywhere else than in the past. Who would have believed that . . . [such regionalism] . . . would take new life in the dynamic and technically integrated post-industrial era, while one no longer hears of the ideologies of the One World of the 'Mondialistes' of twenty years ago?" (p. 12).

shrift of the past in any attempt to modernize rapidly by sacrificing traditional institutions. Sensitive to the fact that his poise and his identity—as well, of course, as those of his nation—are rooted in the past, he deplores the disregard shown by the futurist for this past, and he seeks instinctively to defend historically rooted tradition against any attempt to replace it with elements of the culture of the enemy, that is of the West, unless he can persuade himself that such elements are already an intrinsic part of his own cultural heritage.

But the apologist by his very stance, of course, often pays indirect tribute to the Western culture against which he defends his own culture, and at the same time he betrays his lack of confidence in his own heritage. Laroui, subtly, touches on an aspect of this ambivalence when he observes that the "clerk" in the context of Islam tends to see the power of the West as due not to Christianity, but to the liberal tradition which he claims is implicit or potential in his own religion, Islam.[39] He thus is a liberal when he considers the West, but religiously orthodox when he considers his own people and culture. This double consciousness leads him to defend the religious *status quo* at home and to favor anticlericalism abroad. He will, for example, at one and the same time approve of the inferior role of women at home, of which he cannot help but be conscious, while pointing with glee at reports of the exploitation of women in the West, at the institution of the mistress in France, or the frequency of

[39] Laroui, *op. cit.*, pp. 39-45.

divorce in the United States. He will thus defend a heritage which allows for polygamy at home, and at the same time he will criticize the West for being in fact, if not by law, polygamous.[40]

But the apologist can be more than merely passive to the ills of his society. He can also seek consciously to return to a more brilliant part of his past, or one presumed to be so, and engage in organized political action in this direction. This phenomenon finds expression in movements, often of dangerous potency, such as the Tran Tong Kim of Vietnam, the Ikhwan al-Muslimin (The Muslim Brethren) in the Arab world, the Mahasabha in India, the Pan-Turanian movement in Turkey (today represented by the reactionary anti-Kemalist Nationalist Action Party of the Alparslan Turkeş). Such movements, were they to ever succeed, would doubtless produce results quite radically different from those intended by their partisans, just as the Reformation and the Renaissance in the West, both aiming to restore the purity of a past stage in history, in effect proved to be, each in its own way, revolutionary in introducing manners and institutions that were radically new. Zionism may be considered a case in point.[41]

In the Muslim world the apologetic spirit is particularly apparent. "Muslims," writes Nabih Faris, "are keenly interested in their own history. They live this history and experience its events as though they

[40] See David C. Gordon, *Women of Algeria: An Essay on Change* (Cambridge, Mass., 1968), pp. 29-34.

[41] See Jakob J. Petuchowski, *Zion Reconsidered* (New York, 1966), which makes this point in regard to Israel.

40

were the events of yesterday."[42] He makes the obvious point that the Koran, and the context in which it appeared, can hardly be treated critically because the Koran is the word of Allah himself and as sacred to Islam as Christ is to Christianity. This fact in part explains the Muslim's obsession with the myths of the past, and also, because the great periods of his history were Muslim, that of the secular Muslim Arab nationalist of today as well.

Apologism among Arabs has already been seen in the case of Abdelkader Ben Barka, as it can also in that of the curious polemic of Amar Ouzegane, Minister of Agriculture under Ben Bella, entitled *Le Meilleur Combat*.[43] In a fashion characteristic of so many Arab apologetic historical theses, Ouzegane's book praises French historians who have been sympathetic to Arab culture, Roger Garaudy and Claude Farrère for example, and he denounces those like Gustave Cohen who neglect to show the great contribution of Arabic to French literature, or who praise a Charlemagne who was an imperialist aggressor, according to Ouzegane, against the superior civilizations of Andalusia as well as of Languedoc and Provence. Islam is declared to be a religion of toleration, and the word *troubadour*, claims Ouzegane, comes from *taraba* (in Arabic song, the musical expression of joy and distress).[44] More mod-

[42] "The Arabs and their History," *The Middle East Journal* Spring, 1954: 155-62.

[43] Paris, 1962.

[44] Ouzegane also falls into Morvan Lebesque's gibe in *Le Canard Enchaîné* September 19, 1962: 2, that it now

estly, because he is critical of the decadence, and so
the *"colonisabilité"* of the Arabs in modern times,
Malek Bennabi, in his *Vocation de l'Islam*, similarly
defines a great Islamic past, whose spirit at least he
would have revived.[45] Another example of an Arab
apologist is Omar A. Farrukh, who in his *The Arab
Genius in Science and Philosophy* among other
things cites Gustave Le Bon's statement, "History
has never seen a more human conqueror than the
Arab."[46] Farrukh also argues that the source of
Dante's *Divine Comedy* was Abu al-Ala al-Ma'arri's
Epistle of Forgiveness[47] and includes among the
great "Arabs" of the past the Persian poet and as-
tronomer Omar Khayyam.[48]

One might well question whether historians writing from the apologetic perspective of men like
Farrukh offer much to the progress of Arab society.
They show little evidence of following the pointed
advice of H.A.R. Gibb, for example, that the genuine reconstruction of Arab society on an intellectual
level lies partly in the adoption of a self-critical attitude toward the historical past, in the spirit of Ibn
Khaldun. "Only historical thinking teaches man,"
writes Gibb, "the true measure of his stature and the
humility that curbs theological and scientific arro-

---

seems young Algerians will be taught that the battle of
Poitiers was a victory of barbarism over civilization.

[45] Bennabi has associated himself in sympathy with the
Ikhwan al-Muslimin.

[46] John B. Hardie, trans. (Washington, D.C., 1954), p.
ix.

[47] Ibid., p. 21.   [48] Ibid., p. 39.

gance."[49] This same suggestion that contemporary Arab intellectuals could benefit from the example of their own Ibn Khaldun is also made by Jacques Berque[50] and by Charles-André Julien.[51] Julien introduces his recommendation with a critical examination of Ferhat Abbas' *Manifesto* of 1943 whose "romanticism" he contrasts to Bourguiba's "realism."[52] He criticizes Abbas for talking in terms of the resurrection of a "nation" that has never been; for making Jugurtha an early nationalist; for implying that the Berbers easily accepted Islam (which, in fact, says Julien, they renounced twelve times over a period of seventy years). Citing such assertions as revelatory of the lack of a historical sense among Arabs, Julien observes that Ibn Khaldun failed to become part of the Arab cultural heritage, that it took a Frenchman (W.M.G. de Slane) in the nineteenth century to reveal his greatness.

[49] H.A.R. Gibb, *Modern Trends in Islam* (Chicago, 1947), pp. 126-29. In citing Ibn Khaldun as a model, Gibb has in mind the great fourteenth-century historian's critical scientific objectivity and his "evolutionary thinking," that is, his ability to see that the Muslim polity has changed in the past to meet new problems, and so should be prepared to change in the future, rather than cling to a vain nostalgia for the past.

[50] Jean Stewart, trans., *French North Africa: The Maghrib between Two World Wars* (London, 1962), pp. 373-74. This work is a translation of Berque's brilliant *Le Maghrib entre deux guerres* (Paris, 1962).

[51] *L'Afrique du Nord en marche: nationalismes musulmans et souveraineté française* (Paris, 1953), p. 291.

[52] Ibid., pp. 282-91.

As a final instance of the urge to defend a great past as psychologically necessary in the defense of one's identity one might cite by way of comic relief the case of three Greek journalists who, according to one source, were arrested and beaten as "detractors of our glorious ancestors" and for "a morbid imagination," at the end of 1968 under the regime of the colonels.[53] These journalists were punished not because, in a study of homosexuality among famous ancient Greeks, they questioned the mores of Plato and Sophocles—after all, as intellectuals these were dangerous and effete men in the eyes of the colonels—but because they also dared to implicate Alexander the Great. "Now Alexander," says the anonymous writer of the article in question, "was a glorious military chief, the archetype of the colonels, the model of our governors, who are striving to continue his work. Consequently, suspicion cast on his sexual morality is an outrage to the army."

These various examples of apologetic self-consciousness about the past suggest a defensive and even an evasive attitude toward the challenges of modernity. Such an attitude is not likely to produce objective historiography or to prepare the individual to understand his present culture which, after all, is the product, on the elite levels of society, of an amalgam of the traditional culture and the culture of the colonizer, and, on a popular level, of a historical development which, if not seriously affected

[53] Anon, "Carnets athéniens: un peuple heureux," *Preuves* February-March, 1969: pp. 97-106.

by the influence of the colonizer, has itself moved beyond the culture of the "classical period." Any utopian attempt seriously made to discover "authenticity" by returning to a "golden age" leads to a people's confusion of identity in reverse, both on the level of the educated elite and on that of the masses, albeit for the different reasons that have been suggested.

THE PERSPECTIVE OF THE RECONSTRUCTIONALIST

The term "reconstructionalist" is used only for want of a more convenient one. By it is meant a person who seeks to revive his past, or to defend its greatness, but who at the same time realizes the inadequacies of this past in face of the challenges of modernity. He thus wishes to return to this past spiritually, but only as a basis for the reconstruction of his own society along modern lines.

A person who closely represents what is meant by the term reconstructionalist is the late Jawaharlal Nehru as he describes his spiritual pilgrimage into the history of his people in *The Discovery of India*.[54] Nehru, a highly Westernized Indian Brahmin, educated at Harrow and Cambridge, was initially uninterested in history and negative toward, or at least, alienated from, his own heritage. He says that when he became interested in India as a young nationalist, he "approached her almost as an alien critic, full

[54] London, 1951. All the quotations that follow come from this book, unless otherwise indicated.

45

of dislike for the present as well as for many of the relics of the past that I saw. To some extent I came to her via the West, and looked at her as a friendly westerner might have done." And he adds, "The present for me, and for many others like me, was an odd mixture of mediaevalism, appalling poverty and misery and a somewhat superficial modernism of the middle classes." He was suspicious of the nationalistic pretensions of this class because he felt it had become too much influenced by British culture, and all it really sought was to replace the British in power, not to create anything new or to reconstruct anything authentic.

But gradually he came to feel the need to know this past, initially to him only a "burden" from which, almost like Stephen Daedalus, he sought to awaken. He declares that it was reading Marx that moved him in this direction, to seek a meaning, a pattern in the past useful for an understanding of the present (although he repudiated Marxism as it had found expression in Russia). He came to feel "that the whole of the past belonged to me in the present," that "Past history merged into contemporary history"; it was a "living reality." But his attitude was still negativist, this past was still a *burden*, and he saw its study as something of an exorcism, a sort of psychoanalysis of a people. India's past to him seemed "suffocating" because of its length and its density. But this negative attitude slowly became positive as he assumed his role as a militant in the struggle of Indian independence. "The initial urge came to me, I suppose," he states, "through pride, both individual and national, and the desire common to all men, to resist another's domination and have freedom to live the life of our choice." He wanted to be able to know what India was, what had once given her strength, why she had endured so long, and why, "with a rich and immemorial past," she should find herself in a state of such poverty and degradation. He began to travel over India both physically and spiritually. He discovered among the common people a quality of "gentleness" and "mellowness" that the middle classes lacked. While he deplored their spirit of resignation, he found among the masses a quality of historical continuity, a richness of personality, which linked the present to a past which had survived in spite of all humiliation and domination. He came to feel of India that:

> The hundred and eighty years of British rule in India were just one of the unhappy interludes in her long story; she would find herself again; already the last page of this chapter was being written. . . . For any subject country national freedom must be the first and dominant urge; for India, with her intense sense of individuality and a past heritage, it was doubly so.

While hostile to British rule—the *Discovery* was written in the midst of the struggle for independence—Nehru never sought to gloss over India's inadequacies which had led to her conquest. Somewhere in the past, he concluded, India had lost her "scientific enthusiasm" and she had fallen prey to

47

"irrationalism and a blind idolatry of the past. Indian life becomes a slugglish stream . . . ," while the West became dynamic and progressive. When the British arrived the Mogul empire was in a state of disintegration, loyalties were feudal, there was no "national feeling," and Indians were amateurish and ignorant of the outside world. The British, because of superior organization and discipline, were able to exploit Indian rivalries and disunity, and they were, finally, able to overcome the only serious resistance to themselves, the Marathas.

The effect of British domination was to stunt India's normal evolution, to break the continuum of her historical development, however sluggish it might have been at the time. The British were the only conquerors India experienced who were never culturally assimilated. They maintained an aloof and conservative distance, and discouraged any creative impulse that was genuinely Indian. Nehru denied that India was incapable, without Western stimulus, of having found unity and dynamism on her own. He maintained, on the contrary, that British rule was one of sordid plunder and exploitation, that the "plunder of Bengal" made the Industrial Revolution possible, for example. But Nehru wrote in the heat of struggle. Had he reconsidered the colonial past from a greater distance, judging by the general modesty and balance of his personality as revealed in the *Discovery* and in his *Autobiography*, he would probably have made a fairer judgment of India's colonial past. Be that as it may, Nehru believed that India needed to do much more than attain to independence. She had also to destroy the symbols of a "dead past," to sweep away all the dust that hid India's real beauty and to develop again the "dynamic outlook and spirit of adventure" she had known in the past. Nehru believed that India's personality, reconstructed, would be one to favor world peace and cooperation. But, in any event, he was personally only attracted to the idea of India's playing a great role as she had several times in the past. "No middle position attracted me . . . ," he wrote.

Thus, for Nehru, India's past was to be revived in terms of its flavor, its specificity, its inspiration, but this only insofar as the past was consonant with a creative present. That part of the past which was anemic, which was "burden," was to be eliminated. The reconstruction of India was to involve the return to its historical continuum, but a continuum leading from the great periods of her past to an equally great future that was to be internationalist, and socially and technologically progressive. Nehru was opposed both to the futurist revolutionary approach of the Russians; at the same time, while associated in profound respect and in common cause with Mahatma Gandhi, he was by temperament and ideology impatiently critical of aspects of the traditionalism which Gandhi fostered in their common struggle to rediscover and reconstruct India.[55]

[55] Nehru's ambivalence about Gandhi is made explicit in his *Toward Freedom: The Autobiography of Jawaharlal Nehru*, rev. ed. (New York, 1941), pp. 190-91, 240, 252,

Revealing of Nehru's ambivalence toward traditional India was his declaration in his will that while he denied the act any religious significance, he wished to have his ashes strewn over the land of India and partly in the Ganges, the symbol, he stated, of India's great heritage and of her soul. As André Malraux puts it, there was an English Nehru, but also another, and "even if he did not believe in the divinity of the Ganges, he bore the Ganges in his heart."[56]

Nehru's approach to the destiny of India was, of course, of major importance in setting the guidelines for India's future development. But judging by the enormity of India's problems today, one might wonder whether there was not something remote and Olympian in this approach, as well as something verging on the tragic.[57] One senses this behind the "tired smile" with which he described his

---

316, 318-19. Nehru admired Gandhi for his closeness to the masses and his ability to move them to action, and he felt that Gandhi, "a born rebel," might move instinctively closer to his own social progressiveness as time went on. But Nehru was skeptical of Gandhi's emphasis upon "faith" and his analysis of social reality in terms of "sin" rather than "social forces." Nehru also expresses his difficulty in seeing the institution of religion or the class of the peasantry, with both of which Gandhi identified, as more than reactionary.

[56] *Antimémoires* I (Paris, 1967), p. 356.

[57] See Gunnar Myrdal, *Asian Drama: An Inquiry into the Poverty of Nations* (London, 1969), but also, as corrective, Clifford Goertz, "Myrdal's Mythology: Modernism and the Third World," *Encounter* July, 1969: 26-34.

role in India's history to Malraux,[58] and one suspects a sense of tragedy on Nehru's own part when he contemplated the enormous gap between the modernity for which he strove and the almost stifling reality today of India's cultural heritage, so rich and often beautiful, but also so heavy a mortgage upon the future.

With Nehru in mind, one might question not the sincerity or the ultimate humaneness of the approach of reconstructionalism, but its efficacy, and wonder if in a country like India there might not be a need for the faster, the less tolerant, and alas, the more brutal approach of the futurist. Atatürk may have moved too fast, but Nehru, too slow. Although it is too early to tell, a leader like Bourguiba may turn out to represent a balanced mean.

More generally, while recognizing that each people must come to terms with its particular heritage in its own way, it could be concluded that a modernizing elite, to be effective, should represent both the respect for the past of the apologist as well as the goad and the dynamism of the futurist, the two synthesized by the reconstructionalist with his sense that change, like politics, is the art of the possible as well as of the desirable. But the reconstructionalist approach, to be effective, must be dialectically dynamic and not lead to a paralysis which plays into the hands of the apologist immediately, and ultimately into the hands of the futurist. One shows a disrespect for history at one's peril, but so also is it perilous to limit man to his historicity alone.

[58] Malraux, *op. cit.*, p. 329.

Whatever tendency to softness or compromise the reconstructionalist might reveal, however, he does avoid the paranoiac escapism which tends to characterize both the futurist and the apologist— the former insofar as he imagines he can escape the past, the latter insofar as he imagines he can escape the future. Mehdi Ben Barka sought bravely but vainly to transform a traditionalist society overnight; an Omar Farrukh defends a present by boasting of a glorious past that is radically different from this present—these and the other personalities cited lack the depth, the sense of the tragic, of a person like Nehru who, with all his faults, combined in his vision of India both nationalism and universalism. His position most closely approached what in a later chapter will be discussed as the stage of maturity.

2

THE USES AND MISUSES
OF HISTORY

IN ORDER to help create a national feeling and a sense of unity, as well as to inspire pride and dedication, myths, symbols, heroes, and great events of the past have been resurrected, cultivated, and used to educate the present and future generations of a people. This tendency within the Third World has been nothing new. It has been a repetition and partly an imitation of what Western nations had already done, in the nineteenth century in particular, at the hands of the Thierrys, Guizots, Bancrofts, and Treitschkes.[1] History had already been interpreted to make a French nationalist of Joan of Arc, of Arminius a German; the origin of Spanish kings had been traced back to a son of Noah (Tubal), the British people had been linked to the Trojans, and the making of France had been traced back to the Carolingians. In all of these cases history had been, to one extent or another, abused to satisfy the national ego and to inspire it.

This same phenomenon among those of the Third World in quest of self-determination has been noted and commented upon by many Western scholars of

[1] Among the many books that treat of nationalism and history in the Western context is Boyd C. Shafer, *Nationalism: Myth and Reality* (New York, 1955), which is particularly valuable for its extended bibliography of books and articles on the subject.

modernization and decolonization. Thus, Jean Ches
neaux speaks of a "*réanimation*" that leads the colonized to seek in history the sources of a national
consciousness,[2] and Axelos Abderrahim writes: "The
reanimation of the pre-colonial past is . . . a conse-
quence, but also a pre-condition of decolonization.
In spite of its extravagances, it serves effectively
to reawaken [colonized peoples]."[3] Cyril Black observes[4] that "memories of the heroic past" are
evoked to overcome divisive legacies, to create a
consensus, and where these exist "to overcome significant gaps in the continuum of people and governments . . ." by claiming their ancient civilizations
as "legitimate forebears" (e.g., Turkey, Egypt,
Greece). And David Apter observes[5] that in Africa,
modernizing leaders often interpret changes as the
return to past traditions in order to maintain a sense
of identity among their people, and to justify the

[2] "La Réanimation du passé traditionnel chez les jeunes
nations d'Asie et d'Afrique" in J. Berque, Jean-Paul Charnay, eds., *De l'Impérialisme à la décolonisation* (Paris,
1965), pp. 301-11.

[3] "La Reintegration de soi-même" in Berque, Charnay,
op. cit., p. 352.

[4] *The Dynamics of Modernization: A Study in Comparative History* (New York, 1966), pp. 101-102.

[5] *The Politics of Modernization* (Chicago/London, 1965),
p. 64. Malraux, *op. cit.*, p. 356, observed that many leaders
of the French Community in Africa, even though they
might be Protestants, Freemasons, or Catholics, were also
"great Fetishists," otherwise they would be unable to remain in power.

new by presenting it as a form of the old. For example, the President of Mali before his fall was seen as a descendant of the old Keita royal clans, and Senghor has interpreted the traditional religious forms of Senegal as essentially "humanistic" and "socialistic." Traditional symbols are, thus, employed to make innovations palatable.

This use of history to help to build nations is neatly illustrated in one of a series of articles in *Jeune Afrique*[6] on the possibilities—rather optimistically expressed—of creating a united Maghreb out of the states of Morocco, Algeria, Tunisia, and possibly Libya. According to the writer, Zakya Daoud, an important basis for a Maghreb is the common historical experience of the peoples of these nations, a common experience of conflicts and tensions, to be sure, but in the context of *"un fonds commun de ressemblance."* Common to the North African states, for example, is the experience of the Hilali migration of the eleventh century, of the empire of the Almohads in the twelfth century, and of the heritage of a common colonizer—France. Through the exploitation of this common history in terms of its symbols, Daoud asserts, history can serve, along with other factors of course, to help create a new nation, the Maghreb. It is this impulse to use the myths and symbols of history to help forge national self-consciousness in the struggle for independence and then in the struggle to realize genuine national

[6] "Le Maghreb attend son prophète," *Jeune Afrique* April 28-May 4, 1969: 14-19.

57

cohesion, psychologically as well as physically, that is the subject of the present chapter.[7]

THE COLONIAL ERA

The rise of nationalism within the Third World has occurred, of course, in the context of Western colonialism, and it is not strange that resort should be had to history in order to combat and seek to repudiate the colonial myths which once were employed to justify the imperial regimes. Memmi speaks, in fact, of some of the various myths discussed below as "counter-myths" in refutation of those of the colonizer.[8] Among such myths to be refuted could be mentioned that of France's *"mission civilisatrice,"* the White Man's Burden of Kipling, America's Manifest Destiny, and Hitler's racial theories.

From the point of view of myth, particularly galling to the indigenous of North Africa, for example, were the celebrations in 1930 of the centenary of the conquest of Algiers, held at great expense and with an absurd extravagance, and the simultaneous Eucharistic Congress held in Tunis in honor of St. Louis who had died there during a Crusade.[9] De-

[7] In Karl Deutsch's vocabulary, *op. cit.*, p. 71, symbols, as historical memories, are among the "communication facilities" which enable a people to understand one another and so form a basis for concerted action. Such symbols are also, of course, a way of dividing peoples from one another as symbols and memories differ.

[8] *L'Homme dominé*, pp. 20-21.

[9] See Gordon, *The Passing of French Algeria*, pp. 18-20.

scribing the Algerian centenary, its general director, Gustave Mercier, gave expression to the French myth in stating the purpose of the celebrations to be "To recall (*faire revivre*) an entire century of heroic deeds, leading to the magnificent unfolding of an African France which, born at Sidi-Ferruch [where the French first landed] on June 14, 1830, now stretches from the borders of the Ocean to those of [the gulf of] Syrte, from the Mediterranean to the Congo . . . ," and to demonstrate "the profound and indissoluble union of populations of different origins in a common love of a Fatherland whose generosity and nobility all understand—the irreductible fanaticism of yesterday having given way to the comprehension of a superior ideal, one inspired by the spread [*rayonnement*] of French thought. . . ."[10] Such examples of Western hubris could be multiplied for all of the Western empires, of course, as can examples of the "counter-myths" of the colonized.

But with independence, is the record of the colonial period to be seen only in negative colors? One might entertain as a hypothesis that as self-determination becomes increasingly real and psychological self-confidence replaces "alienation" and the verbiage of propaganda, a balanced attitude toward the good and the bad of the colonial periods will be adopted. Such a development, in turn, might be regarded as the touchstone of genuine self-

[10] *Le Centenaire de l'Algérie: exposé d'ensemble*, 2 vols. (Algiers, 1931), I, pp. 9-10.

determination, of what, for purposes of convenience, will be called "maturity."

The categorical rejection of the idea that the colonial period was anything but one of sterile exploitation has been made by liberal minded Westerners as well as the leaders of the colonized peoples, and often reveals more of a crisis of conscience than a serious and balanced consideration of the evidence. Quite rightly, L. S. Stavrinos takes such a Western writer to task for his thesis that Western imperialism was just one more case of "Extermination, eviction, enslavement, economic exploitation, racial discrimination, injustice, violence, and iniquity. . . ."[11] Stavrinos, in rebuttal, quotes Sir Henry Maine in *Village Communities in the East and West* (1880), writing of India in the 1860s:

> British power metamorphoses and dissolves the ideas and social forms underneath it, nor is there any expedient by which it can escape the duty of rebuilding upon its own principles that which it unwillingly destroyed . . . we do not innovate or destroy in mere arrogance. We rather change because we cannot help it. Whatever be the nature and value of that bundle of influence which we call Progress, nothing can be more certain than that, when a society is once touched by it, it spreads like a contagion.

[11] A review of William Woodruff's *The Impact of Western Man: A Study of Europe's Role in the World Economy 1750-1960* (New York, 1967) in *The American Historical Review* December, 1967: 440-41.

Surely no account of the colonial periods can neglect the implications of such a statement. Nor can one ignore the implications of a remark made by K. M. Pannikar in regard to India, that before the era of nationalism there existed no "historical consciousness," and that the uncovering of India's past was mainly the work of Western historians and archaeologists. Thus it was colonialism which brought into being the sense of history which Pannikar believes to be the *sine qua non* of the spirit of nationalism.[12]

Among the colonized and ex-colonized, it is only extreme apologists, certainly not the "reconstructionalists" or "futurists," who adopt a completely negative attitude toward the colonial period, but all three types are, of course, deeply critical. Thus Nehru, admitting that the British brought "law and order," does suggest that without the British India might have developed more rapidly than has been the case on her own, that the British raj was essentially conservative and uncreative, and that the poorest areas of India today are those where the

[12] *Asia and Western Dominance: A Survey of the Vasco da Gama Epoch of Asian History 1498-1945* (New York, n.d.), pp. 492-93. Christopher Dawson in "The Relevance of European History," *History Today* September, 1956: 606-15, makes the same point: ". . . it was the West that created Indian nationalism by giving India a new sense of its cultural values and achievements." The credit goes to the discoverers of Sanskrit literature, figures like Sir William Jones, Sir Charles Wilkins, Henry Colebrooke, and Anquetil-Duperron.

British were present for the longest time.[13] Albert Memmi argues, on the other hand, that the debate about the contributions of the colonial period is somewhat sterile because there is no way of knowing how rapidly the indigenous might have advanced had there been no occupation.[14] But in the case of Tunisia, he maintains, society was in "full pregnancy" on the eve of the conquest (1881), witness the fact, for example, of the establishment of the Collège Sadiqi, a school with modern features, several years before the French arrived.

A different twist to his argument appears in the less apologetic economic thesis that while the conquered society was relatively underdeveloped and even undeveloped, colonialism, with its exploitative extension of settlement and of capitalism, by its very nature was destined to unite the indigenous and give them a sense of nationality and, finally, to be forced to give way to the new "nation." This thesis is argued by the Tunisian professor, Paul Sebag, and by the Moroccan professor, Albert Ayache, in their statistic-laden polemics against the colonial system.[15] Ayache summarizes this viewpoint when he says of the French attempt to pre-

[13] *The Discovery of India*, p. 101.

[14] *The Colonizer*, pp. 112 ff. In the Resolutions of the Second African Congress, see *Deuxième Congrès* I, p. 409, it was decided that the demoralization of the slave trade was the cause of the drying up of African creativity that could have led to modern progress.

[15] Sebag, *La Tunisie: essai de monographie* (Paris, 1951), pp. 185, 215; Ayache, *Le Maroc: bilan d'un colonisation* (Paris, 1966), p. 324.

serve its "presence" through "cultural oppression": "Vain attempt because the colonial empire, in upsetting the traditional economic and social equilibrium, liberated forces and produced the very *prise de conscience* it sought to avoid."

Proponents of this point of view would not insist that a "nation" had once been conquered; they would simply argue that the time had now come for the colonizers to get out and let the indigenous modernize on their own. This, in effect, is also the position of Sithole discussed earlier when he declares: "The twentieth-century African nationalism is indeed the child of European colonialism."[16] The evasiveness of the apologists has been already discussed; many of them admit the positive aspects of Western civilization, but the argument is made that these already existed in the past culture of the indigenous.[17] A different sort of evasiveness was described to the author by a Muslim Arab colleague whose field of study is modern Egypt. In the early sixties, on trips to Egypt to do research, he found that it was extremely difficult to have access to many nineteenth-century documents, and that some precious documents were even being allowed to perish (by nationalistically oversensitive custodians) on the principle that Egyptian history really begins

[16] Sithole, *op. cit.*, p. 74.

[17] Thus Malek Bennabi, *op. cit.*, pp. 43-44, gives credit to Western colonialism for having shocked Islam out of its "mystical reveries" so that it could now rediscover the dynamism of what he calls the "pre-Almohadin period," i.e. before the twelfth century.

63

in 1952—because until then Egypt had been dom
inated by foreigners (the Albanian-Turkish dynasty
ending with King Farouk, the British, and then corrupt "neo-colonialist" governments). Such an attitude suggests some images in Orwell's *Nineteen
Eighty-Four*, and recalls the adage that those who
neglect history are fated to repeat it.

A case of decolonization that has impressed both
French and Anglo-Saxon scholars as particularly
successful is Tunisia.[18] It has been argued that
Tunisia was colonized for just the right amount of
time to enable a viable and creative synthesis of the
French and the Arabic legacies to be made, and that,
as a result, Tunisia today enjoys relative homo-
geneity, stability, liberality, and is well on its way,
in spite of limited natural resources, toward genuine modernization.

The Algerian writer Abdallah Mazouni pays Tunisia a handsome compliment, in this respect, in a
contrast between Tunisia's and Algeria's problems
of language and identity. Because of their country's
particular historical development, Mazouni writes,
"The Tunisians, always known and recognized as
Arabs, are not, in general, either traumatized or
neurotic [*complexés*]. French culture can be for
them, to a considerable extent, a complement. It
does not menace either their identity or their cul-

[18] See Leon Carl Brown, "Colonization—A Second Look,"
Institute of Current World Affairs (Tunis), May 23, 1961,
and the first part of Charles A. Micaud, with Leon Carl
Brown and Clement Henry Moore, *Tunisia: The Politics of
Modernization* (New York, 1964), pp. 3-66.

ture. At ease as French-speakers and as Arabic-speakers or bilingualists, the Tunisians have no reason to fear, in general, a dangerous invasion by the French language, or any alienation [*dénaturation*]."[19] This is because, he explains, Tunisia was only a protectorate, and the Tunisian bourgeois class was never disrupted and destroyed as its counterpart was in Algeria.

Only the future, particularly the future following Habib Bourguiba's brilliantly competent leadership before and after independence, will tell if this optimism is justified. But, in any case, in regard to its historical self-image and particularly in regard to its attitude toward the colonial period, a touchstone in the present context, Tunisia can be called relatively "mature." Following Bourguiba's inspiration, after his disillusionment with the Arabist romanticism he found in Cairo, Tunisia has opted, in its educational system and in its cultural propaganda, for the notion that it partakes of "Mediterranean civilization," not only of Islamic and Arab civilization, and that, accordingly, it can be proud of its Roman, Carthaginian, and French heritages, as well as of its Muslim and Arabic heritage.[20] It can, thus,

[19] Mazouni, *op. cit.*, pp. 36-37.

[20] Michel Lelong gives Tunisia high marks for cultural openness in "III—Le Résurgissement de la culture nationale en Tunisie" in Ch. Debbasch, *et. al.*, *Mutations culturelles et coopération au Maghreb* (Paris, 1969), pp. 17-40. He states: "Thus, in the present perspective of Tunisian education, Arab culture is not the prestigious vestige of a completed past, offering a refuge for vain nostalgias. It appears,

65

freely borrow from others without feeling that it is threatening its identity or running any danger of "alienation." Bourguibism, in this respect, represents a victory over the attitude embodied in statements once made by the Tunisian writer Ali Belhaoune (who has since these statements were made in 1948 rallied to Bourguiba's cause): "Oriental Tunisia naturally tends toward the Orient. . . . To the modern world the Orient gave Gandhi and the West, Hitler. . . . We still think that it will be the Orient that will save humanity. . . . The misfortune of Hitler was to say aloud what each people of the West thinks of itself."[21] These statements might be

---

rather, as one of the aspects of universal human civilization and as a living tradition from which one must draw inspiration in order to live today and to prepare for the future." For Bourguiba's views of Tunisia's past, as well as of the function of history as a source of national cohesion and progress, see "Value of Historical Studies," a speech delivered at Le Kef, March 12, 1964 (English version distributed by the Secretariat of State for Cultural Affairs and Orientation, April 16, 1964). Incongruous, considering his critical attitude toward the more remote past, is Bourguiba's quite egocentric view of himself as virtually the sole creator of a modern Tunisia which he sees as having transcended the superstitions and the anarchy of the past.

[21] In *Mission* quoted in Clement Henry Moore, *Tunisia since Independence: The Dynamics of One-Party Government* (Berkeley, Los Angeles, 1965), p. 51*n*. This was the spirit that characterized the first important Tunisian anti-French polemic tract *La Tunisie martyre: ses revendications* (Paris, 1920), possibly by Abdelaziz Taalbi, Bourguiba's leading rival to leadership of the neo-Destour during the thirties.

contrasted with those current today in various official Tunisian publications and which have official sanction. Today Tunisians, according to Michel Lelong, a lifelong student of Tunisian culture, denounce *"arabisme fermé et agressif"* with its *"culte du verbe"* and its *"vaines nostalgies."*[22] In *Action* (March 31, 1968), Bourguiba is quoted as saying of the Middle Eastern Arabs: "They have another mentality, they live by sentiment, by passion, sometimes in the unreal." And, to give a final example, Chedly Klibi, Secretary of State for Cultural Affairs and Information, is quoted in *Action* (February 18, 1967), as saying: "We are first of all an Arab Muslim people, but we are also a people that has its Roman history, and its Phoenician and Carthaginian history. . . ."

The attitude represented by the younger Belhaoune—whose themes were used tactically by Salah Ben Youssef, until his assassination Bourguiba's leading political opponent—has been forced underground in contemporary Tunisia.[23] But it is still

[22] Lelong, *op. cit.*, pp. 35-36.

[23] Friendly observers of the Tunisian scene were disturbed by the prison sentences that followed demonstrations and riots partly in reaction to the events of June, 1967, in Palestine. In September, 1968, and February, 1969, severe sentences of one to eleven years were imposed on students and some professors. The accusations made against those found guilty indicate the apprehensions of Tunisia's present rulers in regard to ideological dangers lying in Tunisia's "sub-conscious." As well as for dangerous Marxist tendencies, the demonstrators were reproached for connections with the Ba'ath party (in power in Syria and

thcrc, in Tunisia's subconscious—a potential threat, and it remains to be seen whether the fusion of the heritages of the pre-colonial and the colonial will hold, or whether the pre-colonial subconscious will someday erupt as a conscious and regressive force, as seems to be partly true of contemporary Turkey.[24] To date, in any case, Tunisia has met the test of maturity in so far as it has been able to view the colonial period realistically as a period which, with all its bitter memories and frustrations, nevertheless has become a part of Tunisia's heritage and has contributed to her modernization.

It is more typical, however, than is the case with Tunisia's elite, for intellectuals and publicists of the newly independent nations to tend to view the colonial period—the most sensitive period of a people's historical heritage—only negatively, as a period whose memory is to be exorcised in the struggle to recover their historicity, to restore the historical continuum they feel the colonialists have inter-

---

Iraq) whose "destructive ideology" the Tunisian Press Agency declared to be the cause of so much harm in the Middle East. The most severe sentence fell upon Ben Jennet, a student of Muslim theology, apparently for connections with the Ba'ath party. He was given twenty years of hard labor for his activities on June 5, 1967. The Tunisian press felt it to be significant to observe that a considerable number of those sentenced were educated in traditional religious subjects rather than modern ones. See *Le Monde*, February 23-24, 1969.

[24] See David Hotham, "Democracy in Turkey sits on a razor's edge," *The Times* (London), May 27, 1969.

rupted. In this restoration—this reanimation—the symbols of colonialism are totally rejected, to be replaced by those drawn from the history of the colonized. Thus heroes, for example, of the pre-colonial era are exalted, as are those who combated the colonizer.

EXAMPLES OF HISTORICAL REANIMATION

It is perhaps fair to assume that the specific characteristics, the particular virtues of the hero a people picks from its past to honor, to employ as a model for its youth, to ceremonialize, are some indication of the personality a people aspires to, the values they cherish, even while admitting that the hero as national symbol remains also the same universal hero with a thousand faces.[25] With this assumption in mind, some of the heroes of the past revered by some of the peoples of the Third World treated in this study are now considered, heroes whose names are battle cries in the period of revolution, and heroes whose names become the titles of streets, public parks, and institutions, as well as the protagonists of history school texts, in the period of independence.

[25] Thus A.J.P. Taylor suggests as an index of Germany's self-image, at any one time, the interpretation of Bismarck current among German historians, and he suggests that Goethe as symbol is dusted off when Germany is in trouble. *Europe: Grandeur and Decline* (London, 1967), p. 91. Similar tests in the case of Russia are Peter the Great and Stalin. One need hardly add that for France it is Napoleon, for which see Pieter Geyl, *op. cit.*

The North Vietnamese have named individual military offensives by the names of national heroes like Tran-Hung-Dac who defeated the Mongols in the thirteenth century; and Pan-Turanist Turks have adopted Jenghis Khan and Hulagu (although they were Mongolians) as national heroes to link their history to a great pre-Islamic past.[26] In the Black African context heroes include Samory, who fought the French from 1881 to 1898, Chaka, the great Zulu warrior and tactician, as well as the opponent of the Zulus, the Basuto, Moshesh. And among contemporary leaders Touré has sought to enhance his prestige by claiming a symbolic descent from Samory.[27]

Some of these heroes, of course, are figures of a distant past and because so little is known about them they can assume fanciful epic proportions. For this very reason, however, they tend to be psychologically remote and to serve as rhetorical symbols rather than as effective models and inspirations. The more palpable, because relatively contemporary, heroes—Samory, for example, or the Emir Abdelkader of Algeria who both fought the same foreign enemy as have contemporaries—are probably more viscerally effective as symbols. This

[26] Chesneaux, *op. cit.*

[27] Of Sekou Touré's claim to be Samory's "descendant," Aimé Césaire explains that this is not puerile vanity, but that in so far as Touré "assumes" Samory "he reestablishes" the historical continuum the "accident" of colonialism has interrupted. *Deuxième Congrès des écrivains et artistes noirs*, I, p. 121.

is so, one might suggest, because while close in time, they are also sufficiently distant not to evoke feelings of rivalry and envy. They are recognizably human, but not so close that over-familiarity might diminish the excitement of their legendary accomplishments. But if this hypothesis is true in general, it must allow for the exception of distant heroes whose charisma derives from the religion of a people—heroes who are ever present in the lives of the practitioners of the religion, and whose contemporary potency as symbols is multiplied when religious sentiment is reinforced with nationalism.

Among the Arabs in general the great figures of Islam at its high peaks of civilization are emphasized, Muhammad above all, even by a Christian pan-Arabist like Constantine Zurayk, as are also the early Caliphs, successors to the Prophet who conquered an empire.[28] In later times, a name that constantly appears in nationalistic discourse is that of Saladin to whom the same qualities are attributed as by Western writers like Sir Walter Scott, those of the cultivated, tolerant, gentlemanly warrior. But, of course, to the Muslims part of his grandeur lies in his role as the effective opponent of the Crusaders.[29] The Arabs have a particularly rich religious

[28] Albert Hourani, *Arabic Thought in the Liberal Age 1789-1939* (London, 1962), pp. 309-10. Zurayk sees Muhammad as the creator of Arab culture and the first unifier of the Arabs.

[29] Ibn el-Assal (pseud.), "Return to Cairo," *Encounter* August, 1969: 76-86, suggests the idea of the "anti-hero" as symbol when he talks of the enemies of Nasser as seeing

as well as cultural heritage from which to draw. Heroes also include *Kulturhelden* like Ibn Khaldun, Avicenna, and Rābi'ah, the mystic.

One Arab people in particular, the Algerians, have a relatively recent hero to refer to and to cultivate, Abdelkader, a man whose renown, while being common to Arabs in general, belongs in particular to the Algerians. Thus, as a gesture of ideological solidarity, it was not strange that the ashes of Abdelkader should be presented as a gift by the Syrians to the Algerians, to be buried in Algeria on July 5, 1966, the day celebrating Algeria's independence (1962). The popular significance of this burial of the man who had so valiantly fought the French from 1832 to 1847, and who had attempted, with some success, to establish an Arab kingdom based upon the precepts of Islam, can be judged by the tenor of the special issues of almost all of Algeria's publications devoted, at this time, to Abdelkader. In speeches made on the occasion, the Minister of Foreign Affairs, Abdelaziz Bouteflika, saw Abdelkader's ashes as now properly lying among the martyrs of liberation who had completed the task Abdelkader had started; this, he said, represented a reunion of the Algerian people with their Islamic and Arab history.[30] (Parenthetically, he saw this triumph as evidence that Palestine, also, would be

him as a Khedive Ismail—the ruler who almost literally sold out to the Europeans. The parallel is to Egypt's present-day dependence on Russian aid.

[30] *El-Djeich* (Algiers) July, 1966: 1-3, 6-9.

liberated.) The President of the Council of the Revolution, Colonel Boumedienne, said much the same, and made a particular point of emphasizing that the resistance of men like Abdelkader since 1830 proved that there had been an Algerian nation all along, one now enjoying a "renaissance." And with Boutetlika, the editors of *El-Djeich* emphasized the modernism and progressiveness of Abdelkader, who had disciplined the various tribes by organizing them into eight *khalifaliks*; placed his administrators, *khalifa, aghas, caids,* and sheikhs on regular salaries; combated superstition-ridden fraternities; and sought to undermine "feudalism."[31] The historical validity of this view of Abdelkader as the first great Algerian "nationalist" and modernizer will be considered in a later chapter. But one might remark that in Abdelkader the Algerians have a hero of genuine stature, a man so recognized by most French historians and, during his own lifetime, by the government of Napoleon III, which provided for his honored retirement in Damascus after his defeat and imprisonment. Abdelkader was a very effective military leader, a man who did attempt to create a state based on moral and, considering the period, rational values. He was also a man of culture, a poet and something of a religious philosopher, whose toleration and humaneness were revealed in his treatment of French prisoners, and later in his courageous role as protector of the persecuted Christians in Damascus during the massacres of 1860.

[31] Ibid., pp. 14-15.

Internecine warfare during and following the Revolution has prevented any consensus as to the heroism of the various leaders of the Revolution except for those who died as "martyrs," such as Mourad Didouche whose name has been given to Algiers' main avenue, the former rue Michelet. But clear-cut historical heroes in the safer, more remote, past include figures like Jugurtha and Massinisa who fought against the Romans (the French of the past), and, somewhat ironically, Kahenna, who died fighting against the Arabs in the seventh century, but advised her sons before her death to join the Arabs, and so assured her right to a place in the Algerian pantheon.

In a very different context, the American Black nationalist, in his contemporary quest for a history, unless he seeks for heroes in Africa, or from among the combatants in the contemporary arena—the Malcolm X's and Eldridge Cleavers—is limited to a relatively small number of choices. One of these has become Nat Turner, at least since his name and memory were made famous by William Styron in his *The Confessions of Nat Turner*, a novel approved of by liberal whites almost as deeply as it has been condemned by Black Nationalists.[32] In the

[32] Styron's book was published in New York in 1967. The most severe attacks upon it appear in John H. Clarke, ed., *William Styron's Nat Turner: Ten Black Writers Respond* (Boston, 1968). A searching review of the latter appears in *The New York Review of Books* September 12, 1968: 35-37, by Eugene Genovese. The only outstanding negro writer, to

polemic tract *William Styron's Nat Turner: Ten Black Writers Respond*, the chief objection made universally and unqualifiedly by the Negro writers to Styron's treatment was that it turned this leader of a slave revolt (in 1837) into a sexually ambivalent, over-sensitive, and so ineffective person. Thus, the claim made is, Styron perverted history to suit the needs of the white psyche, and denied to Negroes a historical hero. As evidence for the accusation that Styron has deliberately abused history, some of the black authors observed that Styron fails to indicate that Turner was probably married to a Negro woman and, therefore, they imply rather illogically, could not have become obsessed with a white woman, as Styron claims.

The historical evidence on Nat Turner's uprising is skimpy and, of course, Styron, even if he did refer to the work as a "meditation on history," was exercising the license of the imaginative novelist, but in the interest of mutual understanding and reconciliation between the whites and the blacks, naturally. The almost total rejection of Styron's imaginative reconstruction by the black writers, and their distrust of his motives, is evidence enough of the sometimes alarming importance the historical hero as symbol can have. Of Styron's book, Lerone Bennet Jr. states: "What is this if not a project of

the author's knowledge, to defend Styron has been James Baldwin who declared the book to be the "beginning of our common history." (Quoted in Clarke, *op. cit.*, pp. 31-32.)

75

destruction involving the vitals of the historical personage named Nat Turner?"[33] Vincent Harding entitles his essay "You've Taken My Nat and Gone," while Charles V. Hamilton declares: "Black people today must not permit themselves to be divested of their historical revolutionary leaders. . . . Nat Turner . . . our hero . . . had a profound respect and love for his fellow blacks and . . . respected black womanhood."[34]

Historical veracity in these various cases of history as hero-worship may be suspect; but to the Arabs, a Saladin, to the Africans, a Chaka, to the Algerians, an Abdelkader, and to the Black Nationalists, a Nat Turner, are potent historical figures, models for the young as well as inspirations to the militant. For the future of these various peoples, these heroes have an additional significance. The values they embodied, for good and for bad, become part of the heritage, and so part of the cultural personality of the nation in gestation.

Potent also as symbols recovered from the past are charged words and even languages. Thus, for example, Nkrumah used the title *Osagyefo*, symbolizing his role as crusader or *Mujahid* devoted to freeing Africa from its conquerors, and as Abdallah Mazouni suggests, for Algerian rebels, Arabic "assumed a value as a symbol and a manifestation of another way of life, in face of a colonizer who decreed annexation and preached assimilation."[35]

In the case of Turkey, whose thrust to independ-

---

[33] Clarke, *op. cit.*, p. 11.

[34] Ibid., pp. 74, 78.   [35] Mazouni, *op. cit.*, p. 59.

ence from its Islamic and Ottoman cocoons, as well as from foreign powers, involved mythically a search for pre-Islamic and non-Arabic or Persian symbols, the word "Turk" itself became a symbol. This term had been used in a somewhat pejorative sense before the nineteenth century to designate uncultured peasants—the educated Turk was an Osmanli, a citizen of the Ottoman empire. But with the resurrection of pre-Islamic Turkish history—first at the hands of foreign scholars, and then at the hands of Turks, Ziya Gökalp in particular—the words *Türk* and *Türkiye* finally came to refer, in an honorable and proud sense, to Turkish-speakers whose history extended back to pre-Islamic days, and whose nation included, for the pan-Turanists at least, all Turkish-speaking peoples reaching across southern Russia, as well as Asia Minor. To represent this nation (*Turan*), Gökalp used among other symbols that of the *Kızıl Elma*, the red apple, as title of one of his extravagantly patriotic epic poems.[36] Conversely, symbols like the Caliphate, the administrative authority of the Ottoman sultan inherited distantly from the Prophet, came under attack as representing links to a past to be shed, in this case the Islamic Ottoman Empire. Another symbol, first employed in a new sense by the poet Namik Kemal, was the term *vatan*, whose use had

[36] See Uriel Heyd, *Foundations of Turkish Nationalism: The Life and Teachings of Ziya Gökalp* (London and Beccles, 1950), and Bernard Lewis, "History Writing and National Revival in Turkey," *Middle Eastern Affairs*. The standard work is Lewis' *The Emergence of Modern Turkey* (London, 1961).

been limited to a man's village, but now came to refer to the motherland in a modern nationalistic sense. To Kemal it meant the whole Ottoman Empire, but with the rise of Turkish nationalism proper it came to refer to *Türkiye*. And to the contemporary Turkish nationalist, the most important symbol of all, as well as the hero *par excellence*, is Atatürk himself, the embodiment of the Turkish Revolution and of the aspiration to national consolidation and modernization to which he dedicated his nation.

As symbol-ridden as any nationalist movement has been Zionism, with the rich lore of the Old Testament to draw upon. A dramatic expression of this occurred when a member of the Rabbinical Court of London, in 1948, upon the coming into being of the state of Israel, sounded the *shofar*, as a sign of the Messiah's arrival. And perhaps no city in the world is more symbol-laden than Jerusalem, for Christian, Jew, and Muslim alike. For the latter two the bitter and tragic contest for possession of this city has been at the heart emotionally of the clashing nationalisms of Arabism and Zionism. The Wailing Wall and the Dome of the Rock are as powerful political symbols as they are religious; the memory of the twice-destroyed Beth-Hamikdash, the Temple, is as great a barrier to the solution of the Jerusalem question as is any other factor; and the fire at the al-Aqsa mosque with the destruction of Saladin's famous pulpit on August 21, 1969, served to intensify anti-Israeli feeling among Muslims in general, not only Arabs.

Incidents in history, or crucial periods in time, can themselves become symbols. Thus, in the case of Israel, on July 7, 1969, the memory of Mount Masada, the site where Israeli recruits are sworn into the army, was dramatically evoked when the bones of twenty-seven martyrs were buried with full military honors after a period of two thousand years. These had been among the eight hundred who in A.D. 73 had committed mass suicide rather than submit to Roman rule. According to the correspondent of the Associated Press, these martyrs were honored "exactly as though they were soldiers who had died the day before."[37] Six years earlier, at the recruitment ceremony on June 19, 1963, Professor Yigael Yadin of Hebrew University had stated:

> Masada has become for us a symbol. The poet's words, "Masada shall not fall again," have become a rallying cry for the younger generation and, indeed, for the whole nation. It is no exaggeration to say that it is thanks to the heroism of the warriors of Masada, as to those other links in the long chain of Jewish valor, that we stand here today as soldiers of the army of a youthful yet ancient people, while all about us are vestiges of the armed encampments of those who wish to destroy us. . . . And we, the offspring of those heroes of a distant past, stand here today ready to restore our whole nation. Happy are we to merit this."[38]

Sympathetic to such fervor inspired by history, Edmund Wilson writes: "This milenniarian spanning

[37] *The International Herald Tribune* July 8, 1969.
[38] Quoted in Edmund Wilson, "A Reporter at Large: The Dead Sea Scrolls: 1969—III," in *The New Yorker* April 5, 1969: 45-94.

mixture in Israel of ancient and modern history makes it, in my opinion, a place of unique interest and of heartening inspiration."[39]

In resistance to such pretensions to historical claims to Palestine, Arabs often invoke the symbol of the Crusades which, after long Muslim resistance, met final defeat in the late thirteenth century. Through patience and unity, the point is made, the Arabs can once again triumph over Israel, today's unwanted alien imposition. This use of the memory of the Crusades was made by President Nasser in a speech on October 10, 1960, and by the influential editor of *al-Ahram*, Muhammad Hassanain Haykal, in an editorial on August 23, 1968.[40] In a different context, according to a witness, a well-known Muslim professor of history remarked bitterly during the beginning of a commencement at the American University of Beirut, as the colorful procession of professors made its way to the platform, "Whenever I attend this ceremony, I can't help but remember the Crusaders."[41] In this case, of course, the Crusad-

[39] Ibid., p. 94.

[40] Y. Harkabi, *Fedayeen Action and Arab Strategy*, Adelphi Papers 53, December 1968, Institute of Strategic Studies, London, pp. 5, 32-33. Ibn al-Assal, *op. cit.*, reports that on all levels of discourse, the analogy of the Crusades was common currency in the Cairo of 1969.

[41] The man in question, Omar Farrukh (along with M. Khalidy) in *Missionaries and Imperialism* (*Al-tabshir walistiʿmār*), 2nd ed. (Beirut, 1957), explicitly described St. Joseph, the French Jesuit university of Beirut, and the American University of Beirut as the devils of deculturization. The American University, even in encouraging Arabism, did so in a devious way. It encouraged *secular* Arab

ers were not military invaders, but, to this professor, even more dangerous cultural invaders of the Arab's linguistic and cultural heritage.

As important as any myth in the contemporary Third World, the Arab world in particular, is the Algerian Revolution. Algerians sometimes refer to their revolution as the *Thawrat al-Malyoun Shahid*, the Revolution of a Million Martyrs.[42] This Revolution as an inspiration to the African world may be fading now that its prestige has been marred by the internecine conflicts that have plagued post-independence Algeria, but it continues as an inspiration to Palestinians, particularly the *Fidayeen*, for whom it has been something of a model for obvious, if not always realistic, reasons. The Algerian Revolution thus joins the defeat of the Crusaders as a source of historical inspiration.

As incidents in the remote past can have symbolic potency, so also, of course, can incidents con-

---

nationalism and so sought to alienate Arabs from Islam! Sélim Abou discusses such literature in *Le Bilinguisme arabe-français au Liban: essai d'anthropologie culturelle* (Paris, 1962), pp. 198-205.

[42] The actual figure was most probably considerably under one million but this kind of myth is very difficult to shake. Pierre Beyssade, *La Guerre d'Algérie 1954-1962* (Paris, 1968), p. 255, would place the figure closer to 141,000. Militant Palestinian friends of the author show considerable interest in factual questions of this sort. To them the Algerian Revolution is, of course, a possible model for their own struggle against Israel. The author's own views of the Algerian Revolution appear in *The Passing of French Algeria*.

temporary to those who directly or indirectly have experienced them. Thus, for example, to black South Africans, the events of March 21-22, 1960, in Sharpeville (now by itself a militant term) have become part of a nationalist mythology, recalling the death, according to one report, of over seventy and the injury of hundreds at the hands of the South African police during an unarmed protest march led by the Pan-Africanist Conference to protest discriminatory press laws.[43] And for contemporaries to other such incidents, be it the Alamo or the Bastille, the incident became the symbol over night.

It hardly needs to be said that such incidents which assume symbolic import often cannot withstand much scientific scrutiny, and belong to the realm of mythology rather than fact, although this does little to detract from their potency. If Josephine Tey is correct in *The Daughter of Time*,[44] Richard III had nothing to do with the assassination of his two young nephews—the accusation was part of the "Tudor myth"; and the "Boston Massacre" of March, 1770, according to one informed account, was a case of harassed and provoked British soldiers in a highly tense situation who, almost accidentally, began firing in self-defense.[45] Doubting the "myth," John Adams courageously undertook the defense of the arrested British soldiers, and saw them through to their acquittal.

[43] Kohn-Sokolsky, *op. cit.*, p. 136.

[44] London, 1954; first published in 1951.

[45] Catherine Drinker Bowen, *John Adams and the American Revolution* (Boston, 1951), chs. 20-22.

The mythical use of heroes, terms, and incidents as symbols appears to be an essential part of national reanimation and of nation-building. The remote Saladins and the nearly contemporary Abdel kaders, the semi-legendary Nat Turners, terms like *vatan* and *Türk*, and incidents during the Crusades, all provide grist for the mill of this reanimation. One could hope that when the stage of raw nationalism is transcended these symbols will be desacralized, heroes will be reduced to their just proportions, charismatic terms will be accepted as purely desscriptive, and, when psychic bruises are healed with time, symbolic incidents of "imperialist" oppression against the indigenous peoples of the waning or vanished empires of today will be subjected to critical examination in the spirit of Tey's detective and of John Adams.

TEXTBOOKS AS MEDIA OF REANIMATION

The textbooks of newly independent nations abound in references to their heroes and make use, inevitably, of the symbols of past triumph to inspire, and of past disaster to warn and to strengthen resolve, as has been the case, of course, with Western nations.

Carlton J. Hayes has shown this tendency in the West in his study of the treatment of history in the French educational system since the time, at least, of Jules Ferry.[46] He indicates that in 1923 the Ministry of Education prescribed for the preparatory year (ages 6 to 7) the study of forty lessons (two

[46] *Op. cit.*

and a half hours a week), cach of which dealt with a particular historical hero. Of these forty lessons, only three treated non-French heroes (Franklin, Columbus, and David Livingstone). And in an extensive study of primary- and secondary-school history texts, Hayes concludes that in almost all of them, French genius and civilization are extolled; a sense of service to France is urged; and emphasis is placed on war, on preparation for war, and on military heroes (particularly during World War I for which in most cases Germany is blamed exclusively).[47] In most of these texts, moreover, no basis is given for any criticism of France, for a realization that France has had internal divisions, and little reason is provided for young French students to understand why peoples of other nations could possibly be loyal to their own nations. Until the age of thirteen, Hayes observes, the French child studies his own history almost exclusively; he learns almost nothing of the histories, for example, of even neighboring Italy, Spain, Germany, or Great Britain.

It was this approach to history to which native students of those parts of the former French Empire were subjected. One can appreciate, therefore, the stridency with which *El-Moujahid*, Algeria's official newspaper, announced the beginning of a new curriculum for the *"rentrée scolaire"* of the sixth year of independence.[48] According to the article:

[47] Ibid., pp. 52-55.
[48] September 24, 1968. Quoted in *l'Orient* (Beirut), September 25, 1968.

84

Our ancestors will no longer be Gauls, our children will no longer have to learn this heresy. . . . Our children beginning school this year for the first time, that is those born in 1962 . . . will learn . . . their true history and not the one written by the colonizer. . . . Our children will know that their country could not have been poor, marsh-ridden, and uncultivated since it became France's creditor.[49] . . . [The hearts of the students] . . . will no longer vibrate at the exploits of Joan of Arc but to those of Kahenna, the noble and proud Auresienne who struggled until her death. . . . They will know that their ancestors never accepted defeat and that they always remained upright, courageously defending their belongings, their hearths, and their language.

A revealing study of textbooks in use in the Arab Middle East was made after the 1967 war when UNRWA-UNESCO had to face a crisis which arose when the Israeli Government objected to Arab texts in use in UNRWA schools in territories she had newly occupied.[50] A "Commission of Outside Experts," established to study the contents of these

[49] Algeria was "creditor" because during the French Revolution France became indebted to the *dey* for wheat imported from Algeria.

[50] See UNRWA-UNESCO: Executive Board Reports, particularly "82 EX/8 Paris 4 April 1969: original: English-French" (mimeographed). For a devastating critique of the general hagiolatry and myth-making in many Arab textbooks see Nabih Faris, "The Arabs and their History," *The Middle East Journal* Spring, 1954: 155-62.

texts in light of Israel's complaints, made the final report, the contents of which are discussed in a later part of the present chapter. The Commission studied 127 such books, 70 supplied by the U.A.R. (for children in Gaza), 46 from Jordan (in use on either side of the Jordan River), 11 from Lebanon. Some were in use before 1967, some after, and some were new editions of works already in use. (Syria refused to participate.) The study was made between November, 1968, and February, 1969. The final report was submitted on February 24, 1969.[51] The terms of reference applied are declared to be that while no stand could be taken in regard to the Palestine question, overt exhortations to violence, any appeal for the destruction of a sovereign state, or for the expulsion or annihilation of its people, or any hostile comment applied to a community as a whole are reasons for rejecting textbooks or for insisting upon their modification. Of the texts studied, it was recommended that 48 be readmitted for school use, 14 be permanently withdrawn, and 65 be modified.

Of interest in the present context are the findings of the committee in regard to the historical content of the texts in question. While recognizing the tense psycho-political atmosphere in the area, and while allowing, in part, for the right of a people to interpret history according to national self-interest, the committee made the following observations about those texts it condemned or recommended be modified. In Arabic readers they found an excessive amount of anthology material dealing with the Pal-

[51] Ibid., 82 EX/8 Annex 1.

estine question and much too little about the Arabs' rich cultural legacy in general. In geography texts they observed the word "Israel" was never used, that the area was often referred to as the "usurped portion of Palestine." Emphasis was placed upon the geographical and cultural unity of the Arabs. In texts on Muslim religious instruction, they found too great an emphasis upon the troubles the Prophet had with the Jewish community in Arabia, and some elaborated this to treat the Jews as the perennial enemies of Islam. The symbolic importance of Jerusalem to Christians, as well as Muslims, is treated, but no mention is made of the symbolic importance of this city to Jews. Texts in history and civics sometimes read more like propaganda tracts (for Arabism, and against imperialism and Zionism) than academic sources, they found. Among the historical themes given special emphasis are: the victories of Saladin and Baybars over the Crusaders; the responsibility of the Ottomans for many of the troubles of the Arabs today; the evils of the Sykes-Picot treaty (which involved the partition of the Arab world after World War I), and the glory of the liberation movements of the Arabs. Problems remaining to be solved, among others, are declared to be: the Turkish occupation of the Sanjak of Alexandretta; Mauritania (claimed by Morocco); and, of course, Palestine. The committee noted that throughout many of these history texts, the Arabs are described as victims of the Crusaders, of the Mongols, of Ottoman "despotism," and now of international imperialism and Zionism, and it questioned the wisdom of educating a generation in "so acute an atmosphere of despair, frustration, and antagonism."[52] In the case of even so neutral an area as grammar, the committee found texts which used as examples and exercises sentences such as: "The Palestine army was created as the vanguard of the Arab armies which are struggling to evict Israel and give Palestine back to its rightful inhabitants," and "Imperialism and Israel are endeavoring to weaken the Arabs, who will never rest until they have exterminated their enemies." Finally, the committee objected to the frequent use of terms which at least implied violence: *tahrīr* (liberation), *al-watan al-salīb* (usurped homeland), *al-ghāsib* (the usurper), *tathīr* (purification of the country), and *awdah* (the return).

These cases of Algeria and the Middle East are only some among many examples of the wave of textbook-writing and -rewriting that the end of Western empire has produced. None matches what to an outsider seems to be the historiographical presumption of history texts once used in Turkey. A map appearing in a text used for the first year of the middle school (*orta*) between primary and high school, that was in current use in the years 1947

[52] This despondent view of Arab history is expressed, with regard to Egypt, in Gamal Abdul Nasser, trans. Richard Nolte, "The Philosophy of the Revolution," Institute of Current World Affairs March 8, 1954: 16-18. Egypt's contemporary lack of self-respect, according to the Egyptian leader, goes back to the Crusades which exhausted Egyptian energy and opened the way for the oppression of the Mongols, the Mamluks, the Ottomans, and, finally, the British.

through 1949, is entitled *"Türklerin Anayurdu ve Goç Yollari"* (The Turkish motherland and the migration of peoples"). It has arrows emanating from the area of the Pamir tableland in central Asia and stretching into Europe, the Arab world, India, Eastern Russia, and as far as Indonesia. The Turkish student was meant to understand from this extravaganza that the first civilized people were the Turks, that language began among them in their homeland (*Anayurdu*), and that language and culture spread to the rest of the world along the marked arrows. This is but one unusually pretentious example and illustration of a tendency among newly independent people to manufacture, or elicit from history, self-flattering myths upon which to base their nationalistic aspirations.[53]

THE UNIFYING MYTHS

The Turkish map just discussed is a graphic illustration of what is described by political scientists as a "unifying myth," a myth which integrates

[53] Doubtless many new textbooks will be written to service the new "Black Studies" programs springing up at various American universities. Of great value to these programs will be the mammoth forty-four-volume anthology *The American Negro: His History and Literature* published recently, partly in response to the pressures of the black nationalist movement, by the Arno Press and the *New York Times*. Valuable bibliographical references in regard to black culture in the U.S.A. appear in Marcus Cunliffe, "Black Culture and White America," *Encounter* January, 1970: 22-35. Cunliffe's article also provides a critical discussion of the historiographical issues involved in the black revolution in the U.S.

the various symbols that have been discussed earlier in a total view, providing a people with a comprehensive interpretation of their past in order to inspire them with a sense of destiny. This Turkish case provides a particularly dramatic example.

With the decline of the Ottoman Empire—a decline evident to Westerner and Easterner alike in the early nineteenth century—as Western powers began to pick off different parts of the empire like leaves off an artichoke (Cyril Black's analogy), there developed a form of nationalism, first among intellectuals, which sought to disentangle the Turks from what was now increasingly considered the burden of the Ottoman and of the Islamic past. Advocates of the new view sought to find in the pages of history a Turkey, or a "Turan," as the more extravagant wanted, whose language was Turkish rather than the heavily Arabized and Persianized language of the educated Ottoman, and whose cultural origins were neither Arabic nor Persian. This was found in linking Turkey to the Sumerians, the Trojans, and the Hittites—but not to Byzantium, which was identified, of course, with the rival Greeks. This Turkish nationalism, after it had defined its loyalties in a clear form, distinct from any loyalty to the universal body of Islam and to the moribund Ottoman empire (which had been an international and multi-racial structure), took two essential forms. The one, Pan-Turanianism, envisioned a union of all Turkish-speaking peoples, including all those in Russia. The second, a more moderate, limited, form of Turkish nationalism and the one advocated by Atatürk, and the one which, to date at least, has

90

conquered the field, argued that while the Turks originated in Asia, they came to find their final homeland in Anatolia, and to this homeland they should now limit themselves. They should, according to this second form of nationalism, concentrate upon self-development and abandon any ambitions to expansion that could only lead to trouble with powerful neighbors like the Russians. Advocates of both forms of nationalism, however, agreed that the Turks should abandon any claims to territory occupied by Arabs because any involvement with the Arab world could only deflect Turkey from its proper course, to become a European power.[54]

As formulated by Bernard Lewis, the myth propounded by Atatürk was

> ... briefly, that the Turks were a white, Aryan people, originating in Central Asia, the cradle of all human civilization [the point made in the map described above]. Owing to the progressive desiccation of this area, the Turks had migrated in waves to various parts of Asia and Africa, carrying the arts of civilization with them. Chinese, Indian, and Middle Eastern civilizations had all been founded in this way, the pioneers of the last named being the Sumerians and Hittites, who were both Turkish peoples. Anatolia had thus been a Turkish land since antiquity. This mixture of truth, half-truth, and error was proclaimed as official doctrine, and teams of researchers set to work to "prove" its various propositions.[55]

[54] Heyd, op. cit.
[55] Lewis, "History Writing," 224-25.

Crucial in this extrication from an unwanted past
—the Islamic-Ottoman—and this linking of the Turks
once again to their "true" historical continuum was
the question of language.[56] Under the Ottomans the
educated spoke a very refined language including
many Arabic and Persian words and written in the
Arabic script. The ordinary Turk, looked down upon
as an ignorant boor speaking a primitive language,
was thus culturally segregated from the cosmopol-
itan establishment. Gradually, however, with the
influence of foreign explorers into the past of the
Turks (figures like Lumley Davids who published a
Grammar of the Turkish Language in 1832, the
Hungarian Arminius Vambery, and the French historian Léon Cahun), some Turkish intellectuals
like Mehmed Münif Paşa (died 1910), and then the
Genç Kalemler (Young Pens) in Salonika (founded
in 1911), as well as historians like Suleyman Paşa
(died 1892), began to take an interest in Turkish
and to seek to simplify the cumbersome Ottoman
script (Arabic is unsuitable as script for Turkish, a
non-Semitic language). A leading light, and one of

[56] On Turkey, as well as on other cases of language reform, see Charles Gallagher, "Language Rationalization
and Scientific Progress" in Kalman H. Silvert, ed., *The
Social Reality of Scientific Myth: Science and Social Change*
(New York, 1969), pp. 58-87. Gallagher here is concerned
with language reform as a means of modernization in the
sphere of science, making access to modern terms, over-
coming diglossia, and so forth, easier—in short, with re-
placing "linguistic traditionalism" with "linguistic modernity." In contrast, the present study is concerned with the
political-historical significance of language reform.

the most influential prophets of modern Turkish nationalism, was Ziya Gökalp, who worked with the Young Pens of Salonica and as early as 1909 published poems in the simple language of the people to promote the adoption by all Turks of their authentic national language.[57]

With independence in 1923, under the relentless leadership of the commander of the successful revolution against the annexationist plans of the Great Powers and finally of Greece, the stage was set for the radical series of reforms designed to break, finally, with the Ottoman and oriental past. In regard to language, steps were rapidly taken to "liberate . . . [Turkey's] language from the yoke of foreign languages," as Atatürk once put it.[58] An adapted Latin script replaced the Arabic, and a commission, the *Türk Dil Kurumu* (Turkish Linguistic Society), was established to explore Turkey's historical past and to dig out from the past, or from common speech, words to replace Arabic and Persian terms. In the face of opposition to those who objected that Turkey was cutting itself off from its cultural and religious past, the answer given was the myth already outlined. But as Atatürk and his supporters had to worry about the dangerous extremism of the Pan-Turanians, so also were they concerned with the linguistic purists who sought to extirpate every trace of Arabic and Persian, many of

[57] Heyd, *op. cit.*

[58] Uriel Heyd, *Language Reform in Modern Turkey* (Jerusalem, 1954), p. 191. Atatürk's statement was made in 1930.

93

whose terms had entered common usage, and to deny entry to Western scientific terms. The danger was that excessive purism might create as serious a cleavage between the educated and the ordinary language as had been the case in the Ottoman Empire, and inhibit scientific progress. It was against these possibilities that Atatürk sanctioned one of the most extraordinary historical myths possibly ever devised, the Sun-Language Theory. According to this theory, the first man to utter a human sound did so while looking at the sun, somewhere in central Asia. This first man was a Turk and his first word was "ağ" (ak in modern Turkish, meaning white, bright). With this momentous utterance, the language from which all other languages have been derived was born. Writes the leading authority on Turkish language reform, Uriel Heyd:

The new policy of moderation [against the Purists] was justified by a linguistic theory developed in those days [1935 and after], the Sun-Language Theory. Its defenders claimed that just as Central Asia, the home of the Turkish race, was supposed to have been the cradle of human civilization, so Turkish was the mother tongue of mankind. Many Arabic, Persian and European words used in the Ottoman language were in fact of Turkish origin, and therefore did not have to be eliminated. Thus the eager search for Turkish words to replace those of foreign origin subsided. During the following years the Linguistic Society turned its attention mainly to the Turkification of technical and scientific terms for schools; in 1939 about

94

five thousand Turkish terms were officially introduced into the language of instruction and in textbooks.[59]

That confusion has followed from the transformation of the Turkish language, and that violent controversy has accompanied this transformation, has been inevitable. The Constitution of 1924, to give an illustration, was replaced in 1945 by a reworded constitution, many of whose terms were unrecognizable to ordinary Turks (a glossary had to be appended!) In 1952 it was decided to return to the 1924 version but by then some of the terms in the original constitution had become archaic.[60] And a price, one very difficult to measure, that the Turks have paid for this return, linguistically, to their presumed authentic historical tradition, has been that young Turks today are cut off from a rich literature and heritage. Indicatively, the writings of perhaps the leading prophet of this reform movement, Ziya Gökalp, can be read by young Turks today only with difficulty because of the language gap, and the same is true of Atatürk's famous speech of 1927.[61]

[59] "Language Reform in Modern Turkey," *Middle Eastern Affairs* December, 1953: 402-409. For a representative pamphlet defending the new theory see Muzaffer Muhittin Kalkilic, *Étude sur la Théorie Gunes-Dil*, presented to the Third Congress of the Turkish Language, Istanbul, 1936. As sponsor of the theory Atatürk is declared to be one of the greatest scientific geniuses of all time.

[60] Heyd, *Language Reform*, pp. 44-48.

[61] *A Speech Delivered by Mustafa Kemal Atatürk 1927* (Istanbul, Ministry of Education, 1963).

In this speech, which lasted from October 15 to October 20, Atatürk outlined a destiny for his people that was almost completely "futurist," suggesting that, for him at least, the Sun-Language Theory was little more than a tactic of presumably temporary value. Turkey, Atatürk stated, had to make itself worthy "in the eyes of the civilized world," and to rid itself of institutions like the Caliphate, "a laughing-stock in the eyes of the civilized world, enjoying the blessings of science."[62] A break with the past was needed, he insisted, and he quoted with contempt the statement of a political opponent (Cebranli Kürt Halit Bey): "They are attacking the very principles which perpetuate the existence of the Mohammedan world. . . . The assimilation with the Occident means the destruction of our history, our civilization."[63] Symbol of the past, the fez "which sat on our heads," said Atatürk, "as a sign of ignorance, of fantacism, of hatred of progress and civilization," was outlawed to be replaced by the Western hat, "the customary headdress of the whole civilized world."[64] Turkey, in short, was to be transformed into a "national and modern state founded on the latest results of science."[65]

Without challenging the enormous contributions made by Atatürk to the creation of modern Turkey, one might still wonder if such an uncompromising futurist approach as his might not represent a danger to genuine reconstruction, and to social and psychic stability. As seen, Atatürk and his support-

[62] Ibid., pp. 10, 593.   [63] Ibid., p. 734.
[64] Ibid., p. 738.   [65] Ibid., p. 740.

ers did attempt to fill the historical vacuum that the surgical approach just described has created,[66] but this Turkish myth, represented in its crudest form in the Sun-Language Theory, in itself may not offer the spiritual sustenance provided by the rich and complex heritage of Islam; conversely, it is hardly compatible with the "scientific" approach to life to which Atatürk dedicated his nation.

How far the Turks today with greater national self-confidence have transcended the crude historiography of the immediate past is difficult to determine. Hopefully, Halil Inalcik speaks for many Turkish academicians when he writes that even if the "national view of history" did encourage much historical research, it was "not free from exaggerations," and he expressed disapproval of "nationalistic historiography of newly independent people" whose prejudices often "overshadow historical realities."[67] But here, ironically, Inalcik is referring to Arab historians who disparage Turkey's contributions to Islamic civilization!

Other peoples than the Turks, of course, have seen in language reform a means to nationalistic self-fulfillment, the Norwegians and the Greeks for example. In the case of the latter, Adamantios Korais began the language question when he urged

[66] A parallel case of the tactical use of history by a futurist is the exploitation of the symbols of the myth of "Mother Russia" by Stalin during the dark days of World War II.

[67] "Some Remarks on the Study of History in Islamic Countries," *The Middle East Journal* Autumn, 1953: 451-55.

the Greeks to revive their classical heritage, now "corrupted" by the Turkish overlay, and to reestablish their historical link, as direct descendants, with the ancient Greeks.[68] To do this he advocated an education based on the classics and the use of a language which would be a mixture of classical Greek and the language of the present educated middle classes. He rejected the use of liturgical Greek or of the "debased" Greek of the common people, *demotiké*. This new language, shorn of Turkish terms among others, became the *katharevousa* of today's administration, academia, and of journalism, while everyday Greek remains demotic. Throughout modern Greek history the battle has raged between the proponents of the use of *katharevousa* and those of *demotiké*[69] as the appropriate language of literature and education (as in a different form it has among the Arabs). Progressives like George Papandreou have favored the demotic; the present regime of "the colonels," doubtless because they consider the link to Greece's great ancient past as represented by *katharevousa* a matter of national honor, have purged the educational system of the demotic elements their late *bête noire*, Papandreou, had introduced.

[68] John Campbell and Philip Sherrard, *Modern Greece* (London, 1968), pp. 40-43, 60, 146, 242-43, 388. Language is, of course, a problem for many other nations today, African and Arab countries and India, among others. English, by and large, remains the main avenue to modernity in India, and in many Arab countries and Africa it shares this role with French.

[69] i.e., between "cleansed" or "popular" Greek.

While for the Turks and Greeks the crucial focus of concern in regard to their identity may be considered to have been language, for the Arabs it has been religion. Their historical heritage has seemed to them, understandably, almost one with Islam. Islam is based upon the revelation through an Arab of a holy text, the Koran, in Arabic. Their great moments in the past were those of Islam, their heroes were scholars of Islam, theologians, and warriors of *Jihad*. It has been, and still is on a psychological if not an ideological plane, difficult for the Muslim Arab to distinguish between his national and his religious community. And it was the humiliation of the latter in modern history which has helped to encourage his nationalistic stance. This is partly true because it is in history and through the Muslim community that the realm of the divine—even if this realm is ultimately of transcendent and paramount importance for Muslims as individuals—finds expression on earth.[70] In this respect, Islam is closer to Judaism than to Christianity, which regards political tragedy on earth as more a test and a preparation for the afterlife than as any indication of religious failure. In any case, when Islam in the nineteenth century experienced one reversal after the other with the successful spread of Western Christian imperialism, it was as much as political nationalists as it was as religious reformers that Jamal al-Din al-Afghani, Muhammad 'Abduh, and the other prophets of the *Nahda* (the Arab renaissance) sought to revitalize the Muslim community

[70] W. C. Smith, *op. cit.*

and restore its political initiative.[71] This interrelationship of religious and secular political concern helped to prepare the way for the Arab nationalism of the post-1908 period. Thus Afghani advocated a militant political stance among Arabs, and 'Abduh sought to introduce "reason" and other characteristics of the powerful West into the Muslim community by showing them compatible with Islam at its best and in its brighter past.[72] Rashid Rida and others began to envision the rebirth of Islam in almost identical terms with the rebirth of Arabic culture, and 'Abdal Rahman al-Kawakibi (died 1903) Arabized the movement even more by attacking the Turks as unfit to hold the Caliphate and in seeing the true Muslim community (*umma*) as that of the Arabs, whom he treated as the true leaders of Islam, culturally superior to the Turks. Ultimately, this Arabism became secularized, and men like Sami Shawkat and Amin al-Rihani declared that Arab history begins well before Islam; that it has links with Hammurabi and Rameses; and that the Arabs were

[71] Among the best works on the subject are Smith, *op. cit.*, Albert Hourani, *op. cit.*, Nadav Safran, *Egypt in Search of a Community: An Analysis of the Intellectual and Political Revolution of Egypt, 1804-1952* (Cambridge, Mass., 1961), Sylvia G. Haim, ed., *Arab Nationalism: An Anthology* (Berkeley and Los Angeles, 1964), pp. 3-72.

[72] Malcolm Kerr in *Islamic Reform: The Political and Legal Theories of Muhammad 'Abduh and Rashīd Ridā* (Berkeley and Los Angeles, 1966) treats in part 'Abduh's break with the typical Islamic apologetic spirit while remaining ambivalent in his attitude toward genuine modernity.

100

already civilized people while the Europeans were still living in forests. This shift to seeing Islam as more a cultural heritage than a religion is now common among the various strands of Pan-Arabist nationalism, and it is for this reason that Christians like Nabih Faris, Constantine Zurayk, and many others have been able to identify with the Pan-Arabist cause and in many cases to be important leaders of the movement.[73]

But many other Christian Arabs, especially the Maronites of Lebanon, are suspicious of the claim of Pan-Arabists—today most militantly represented by the Ba'ath party in Syria and Iraq, and by Nasserism in Egypt—that it is possible to separate Islam from the idea of the Arab nation. To these Christians the prospect of a united Arab nation is a fearsome one. Should it materialize, they feel, they would inevitably, as Christians, be treated as second-class citizens. And it would not be unjust to say that while the identification of Muslim and Arab is not true for leading prophets of Arab nationalism like Sati' al-Husri, Zurayk, and others, it doubtless is true for many ordinary Muslims. A small but significant episode an Arab Christian recounted to the author was of a conversation he once held with a group of Egyptian villagers. He found that he was unable to persuade them that the president of the

[73] Hourani, *op. cit.*, p. 308 states: "Rida would have defined Arab culture in terms of Islam: Bazzaz does rather the opposite. Islam is a national religion. . . ." Bazzaz has been a leading Iraqi nationalist ideologist. Chejne, *op. cit.*, has some interesting comments on this subject.

Lebanese Republic was a Christian. They could not imagine, he said, that an Arab nation could be ruled by anyone but a Muslim. While one should not exaggerate the implications of such an incident, still, one should not overestimate the degree to which patterns of mind have changed, nor take at its face value the claim that today the myth of Pan-Arabism has been desacralized.[74]

Deviations from the Arabist myth, among Arabic-speakers, include the Lebanese Christian myth that the modern Lebanese are direct descendants of the Phoenicians (not of the Arabs or of Islam) and, in consonance with the supposed contribution of the alphabet to humanity, are also preeminently civilizers, today of peoples eastward, standing as an advanced "Land of Light."[75] This myth appears in the writings of the poet Said 'Aql and of Michel Chiha, the preeminent ideological prophet of mod-

[74] For an insight into the religious element in Lebanese nationalism, see Dominique Chevalier, "Une Iconographie des Maronites du Liban," *Revue historique moderne et contemporaine* X (1963): 301-308. *Inter alia*, Chevalier reproduces popular religious pictures showing Camille Chamoun, the Bonnie Prince Charlie of many Maronites, within a heart on the bosom of Christ who is pointing a finger toward him, and another showing the Madonna and Child with Mary's arm draped around Chamoun's shoulder. The former was produced during the crisis of 1958 when Lebanon was involved in a partly sectarian civil war and the latter for a religious festival in 1953.

[75] See Nabih Faris, "Lebanon, Land of Light" in James Kritzeck and R. Bayly Winder, eds., *The World of Islam: Studies in Honour of Philip K. Hitti* (London, 1959), and Abou, *op. cit.*

ern Lebanon, among others, and in the declarations of the leader of the paramilitary political party *Al-Kataeb al-Lubnaniat* (the *Phalanges Libanaises*), Pierre Gemayel. Gemayel, in a statement made on the occasion of a homecoming of Lebanese immigrants in 1956 stated that were Lebanon to be absorbed by a larger neighbor (Pan-Arabism, as indicated, is the bugbear of Lebanese Christians, the Catholic Maronites in particular) it "would create insurmountable difficulties for this neighbor, so great is its capacity for resistance and its faith in its own mission."[76] And on this "mission" Gemayel elaborated:

> Since distant antiquity, Lebanon has marched with a giant's feet on the road of civilization. Even while they were only Phoenicians, the Lebanese already showed their sense of the universal, their attachment to liberal traditions, and a generosity of spirit and heart so great that it enabled them to love and understand even the most distant peoples. . . . It is thus that they have contributed to the blossoming of Mediterranean civilization in the domains of art, of science, of religion, and of material progress. Western humanism, a tributary of Rome and of Athens, owes to them its first foundations.

[76] "Six Thousand Years in the Service of Humanity," (Beirut, 1955). This English translation was made by David Gordon from a speech delivered on February 25, 1955. Crucial to the Lebanese myth is the legend that Cadmus, founder of Thebes, brought the Phoenician alphabet to Greece.

103

A different myth is that of the Syrian Social Nationalist Party which rejects the nation of Lebanon as an independent and sovereign state and, instead, sees Lebanon only as a part of Greater Syria.[77] In a statement of party doctrine, Antum Sa'ada, the party's founder and leading ideologist, declared: "The Syrian Nation is the Ethnic Unity of the Syrian People which has developed through a long history beginning before the era of recorded history." This Syria is seen as a geographically determined crucible (it includes Cyprus, the Sinai peninsula, the gulf of Aqaba, and today's Iraq, but excludes Egypt, the Arabian peninsula, and, of course, Turkey and Iran). Within this crucible was fashioned "an original and independent Syrian mentality" that is able to comprehend and assimilate "every science, every philosophy, and every art in the world."

While for the Turks a major aspect of the quest for identity has been the linguistic, and for the Arabs the religious, for Black Africans a crucial aspect has been the racial. The oppressor, the slave-owner, was a white man, and the educated African, treated in general as an inferior being with no proper history of his own, studied until recently the history of white peoples. According to the American black writer Louis Lomax,

[77] Antun Sa'ada, English translation, *The Syrian Social Nationalist Doctrine. The Principles and Aims of the Syrian Nationalist Party. Interpreted by the Leader* (Beirut, 1949).

104

... racism is the irritant on Africa's raw nerves—not colonialism, but that *white* peoples have colonized *black* people; not settler domination, but that *white* settlers have dominated indigenous *black* people; not economic exploitation, but that *white* people have exploited *black* people; not social discrimination, but that *white* power structure sets itself apart from *black* masses; not denial of civil rights, but that *white* people deny *black* people their civil rights.[78]

With the rise of nationalism in Africa, around the time of World War II in any massive sense, African intellectuals began to take an interest in their history, and in the case of the French African empire to assert their "African personality" under the rubric *Négritude*, a term first popularized by two French educated poets, Aimé Césaire (an Antillian) and Léopold Senghor (now president of his native Senegal) in the mid-thirties.[79] In 1947 Senghor and Alioune Diop founded the most important journal to promote this concept, *Présence Africaine*, in Paris. The goal the editors set themselves was, negatively, to combat assimilation (to the West) and, positively, to explore the great periods of pre-colonial

[78] Louis E. Lomax, *The Reluctant African* (New York, 1960), quoted in *Current* February, 1961: 47-52.

[79] The origins of the idea of *Négritude* go back to Edward Blyden, the first president of the Liberian University, and the writer René Maran of Martinique who won the Prix Goncourt in 1921. See Kohn and Sokolsky, *op. cit.*, pp. 72-74.

African history, and to popularize the oral poetry and plastic arts, as well as the representative social institutions, of Africans. The irony of this enterprise was soon pointed out by some Europeans and by some Negro intellectuals who grew up under British rather than French rule: the irony of a group of well-educated men in French culture, whose main market for their poetry was France, rather than Africa, launching a program whose intent was to repudiate the West and to cultivate values presumably unique to Africans, with roots deep in the African psyche and in the African past. This irony can perhaps best be explained in psychological and existentialist terms; it is the non-Westerner who penetrates most deeply into the heart of the West, but without ever being fully accepted, or so he imagines, who most deeply comes to sense his "otherness," and so, by reaction, seeks for his "authenticity" in the culture from which he has been uprooted. He comes to love and cultivate that which his education and training has taught him to reject and disparage.[80] What is black is now seen as beautiful rather than sinister, the "primitiveness" of African culture is now seen to be rich in its closeness to nature and in its sense of the communal (as opposed to Western "individualism"), and a past once seen as non-historical is now seen to be rich in symbols and in accomplishments.[81] The Negro, says Sartre,

[80] Immanuel Wallerstein in *Africa: The Politics of Independence* (New York, 1961), p. 76, makes this point.

[81] In opening the proceedings of the First International Congress of Africanists, President Nkrumah's main point

"now arises, he assumes the word black once hurled at him like a stone."[82] Inevitably, the spirit of *Négritude* is apologetic, and logically it represents a point of view which, if applied literally, as Frantz Fanon and others have argued, is a barrier to progress.[83]

---

was that the chief "myth" African historians had to combat was the notion that Africa had no history. This idea of the rights of a people "with a history" over those allegedly without one has an interesting parallel in the Habsburg Empire in the nineteenth century when Czechs, Germans, and Magyars lorded it over the Slovaks and Ruthenes who, the former claimed, had no history and hence no claims to a separate sovereign status. See Taylor, *op. cit.*, p. 128.

[82] Quoted in *Le Monde*, June 21, 1969, in an article on "La Négritude, mythe ou réalité?"

[83] The case against *Négritude* takes various forms. To Marxists (see Gabriel d'Arboussier, "Une Dangereuse Mystification: la théorie de la Négritude," *La Nouvelle Critique* June, 1949: 34-47), its supporters are "false prophets" who confuse racial issues with the real issues which, of course, for Marxists are economic. Liberal humanists have objected to the racist implications of the doctrine. See Ezekiel Mphahlele, *The African Image* (London, 1962). For Sartre's sympathetic but negative critique see "Orphée Noir" in Léopold Sédar-Senghor, *Anthologie de la nouvelle poésie négro et malgache de langue française* (Paris, 1948), pp. i, ix-xliv, and for Fanon's reluctant acquiescence to Sartre's critique see his *Peau moire masques blancs* (Paris, 1952), pp. 134-35. At the recent Pan-African Festival of Arts held in Algiers in July, 1969, supporters of *Négritude* from the French-speaking African states were thrown on the defensive, doubtless to the pleasure of Arab North African delegates who could only benefit ideologically, when many delegates attacked the idea of *Négritude*. One of the outstanding figures to so do was Sekou Touré. *L'Express*

As an aesthetic principle it has, however, helped to inspire some significant literature, the poetry of Senghor and Césaire, for example, and the novels of Cheikh Hamadou Kane and Camara Laye's brilliant *Le Regard du Roi*. It has also, of course, encouraged an interest in African history and in its exploration, and it can only be regarded with sympathy as an inspiration if it helps Africans to respond to Césaire's invocation: "Let the black peoples take their place upon the great stage of history."[84]

To date, interest in African history has grown phenomenally in the world in general.[85] This interest was already apparent at the First International Congress of Africanists in 1962, which drew 146 African scholars and intellectuals, and 309 from

---

(August 4-10, 1969: 42) described the confrontation as that between Frantz Fanon's view, "One must liberate the man of color from himself," and that of Senghor, "Emotion is negro as reason is Hellenic." On the conference see *Le Monde*, August 5, 1969. According to some observers "Africanism" confronted "Arabism" at this conference and some Africans expressed resentment—in the way prizes were awarded, for example—at indications of a sort of Arab "cultural imperialism." See Jim Hoagland, *The International Herald Tribune*, August 13, 1969.

[84] Kohn and Sokolsky, *op. cit.*, p. 153. The view that *Négritude* is essentially defensive (against depersonalization) and not racist is often defended. See, for example, Jacques Rabenmananjara, at the time minister in the government of Madagascar, in *Afrique Action* March 27, 1961: 22-23.

[85] See Roland Oliver, "Exploring the History of Africa," *Encounter* March, 1963: 34-41, and Charles Patterson, *op. cit.*

other parts of the world. Today, UNESCO plans to sponsor a General History of Africa to contain, ultimately, nine volumes as an international effort,[86] and in African universities scholars like Dr. K. Onwuka Dike have already been working on the reconstruction of Africa's past according to modern critical methods. In spite of the lack of sources and the dependence on oral traditions in many cases (it is said that when an old African dies, a library perishes with him), the reality of African history and its significance are no longer, as formerly, a question of doubt.

Already enough of the past has been uncovered to provide material for pride as well as apologia, and to serve the mythical needs of African nationalists. The "fanaticism" of the Mahdi of Sudan (who killed General Gordon at Khartum) is now open to serious question; there is fresh knowledge of the University of Sankoré in Timbuktu (at which a distinguished sheikh, Ahmad Baba, taught in the sixteenth century); and along with many artistic accomplishments in the past, the complexity and depth of the metaphysics of some African oral literature is now known.[87] Africans can now take pride in the sculptures of Ife and Benin and the castles

[86] *Jeune Afrique* July 14-21: 1969, 58-59.

[87] For positive treatments of Africa's past accomplishments see Janheinz Jahn and Marjorie Grene, *Muntu, An Outline of Neo-African Culture* (London, 1961), first published in 1958; Thomas Hodgkin, *Nationalism in Colonial Africa* (London, 1956), and his "What Future for Africa? I," *Encounter* June, 1961: 3-8.

of Gondar, now objects of international respect, and Ethiopia, because of its ancient and continuing monarchy, its sacred literature, its script, and, of course, because of its triumph over Italy at the battle of Adowa in 1896, has become of symbolic importance to Pan-Africanism.[88]

But the effort to recover Africa's past is difficult, and even more difficult is the task of reconciling the demands of modernism with institutions of the past such as animism and tribalism. Inevitably the impatient African nationalist has often resorted to extravagant and exaggerated claims for his past. The outstanding case of such mythical pretension, one that often evokes smugly bemused comments from Western observers, is the murals in public buildings in Ghana which depict blacks as the inventors of almost every important artifact of world civilization. Sheikh Anta Diop traces the origin of civilization to the Egyptians who, he argues, were blacks, a fact Westerners have taken pains, he says, to obfuscate;[89] Dika Akwa insists that Moses and

[88] Hodgkin, *Nationalism*, pp. 180-81.

[89] The Second Congress of Black Writers and Artists (Rome, 1959) resolved to recommend a systematic consideration of Diop's thesis as to the negroid origin of Egyptian civilization. See *Deuxième Congrès*, I, pp. 387-421, for the resolutions. In *L'Unité culturelle de l'Afrique Noire: domaines du patriarcat et du matriarcat dans l'antiquité* (*Présence Africaine*, 1959, Flers, Ornel), Diop propounded another anti-colonialist thesis when he argued the superiority of matriarchal Africa over the patriarchal and originally "nomadic" West. African optimism is contrasted with Western pessimism.

Buddha were blacks and the sources of the thought of Nietzsche, Bergson, and Marx are to be found in Bantu philosophy;[90] and Diop, at the First International Conference of Negro Writers and Artists held in Paris in 1956, argued that Africa's "regression to tribalism" was provoked by colonialism![91]

It would almost seem that the more tenuous the possibility of linking the present to a great past, the more extravagant the myth. It is appropriate that E. U. Essien-Udom, in his study of Black Nationalism in the United States,[92] should use, as indicated earlier, the term eschatology rather than myth for the vision of history entertained by the Black Muslims and other black groups in America. The term myth suggests some connection, however remote, with verifiable historical reality, while the historical reconstruction of the Black Muslims, among others, can only be seen, and only defended, in terms of revelation. Briefly, the eschatology of the Black Muslims, as first revealed by Allah, the Great Mahdi or Messiah, the Son of Man, and the Savior, all alias W. D. Fard, who came to America from Mecca on July 4, 1930 and was the offspring of a platinum blonde and of a jet-black man of the tribe of Shabbaz (a black Asian nation), is that the Black Nation originally lived on the moon (here the symbols of the crescent drawn from traditional Islam). Several

[90] See Jahn, op. cit., and Hodgkin, Nationalism, pp. 129, 173-74.

[91] See Emerson, op. cit., p. 156.

[92] Black Nationalism: A Search for an Identity in America (Chicago, 1962).

111

trillion years ago a black scientist, unable to make all people speak the same language, caused an explosion that separated the earth from the moon. The first people on earth and the founders of Mecca were the blacks, from whom an evil black "grafted" the white people, symbol of all evil. In 1555 John Hawkins began the enslavement of some of the Negroes in America. These Negroes are the chosen people from among the black race. God is now on earth among them and a new civilization is to be born after the Caucasians and Christianity are destroyed. This is to occur sometime before A.D. 2,000, and for this the evidence, prophesied in the Scriptures and in the Koran, is the fact that the white empires are coming to an end, the colored people are asserting themselves (at the Bandung Conference in 1955, for example), and Islam is spreading throughout Africa.

Other black American eschatologies are equally fanciful: the "Abyssinians" trace their origin to Ethiopia; and the "Moors" are "Asiatics" sprung from the Moabites as stated in Genesis 19:37, while the Negroes are the Jews to whom the Bible refers. Theodore P. Ford, in a reversal of the myth of Diop referred to above, sees the American blacks as descendants of the original Egyptians, captured by warlike blacks and sold into slavery.[93] Thus, for him, the American blacks are not of African Negro origin. Inevitably, where peoples are intermingled, historical myths will contradict one another and clash, as do these eschatologies that have blossomed in the

[93] Ibid., p. 130.

tortured racist soil of the "melting pot" of American democracy.

These various myths of Turks, Greeks, Arabs, Africans, and American blacks have been elicited to varying degrees of credibility from history to satisfy psychic as well as political demands. It would seem that the greater the need, the greater the historical insecurity, the more fantastic and pretentious the myth, but each has served, or continues to serve, a historical purpose—each has its own rationale in the psychic and political emancipation of a people. Of the cases discussed, the Turkish myth has helped a people to shed one identity, the Ottoman, in order to assume a new one, the Turkish. For the Greeks it has been a way of recovering self-respect after centuries of alien, Turkish domination. For many Arabs, it is a means to unification, while for many Lebanese Christians it is a way of defending themselves against absorption into the Muslim world. For the blacks of Africa and for American blacks, as heirs to a little known and frequently disparaged history, it is a way of acquiring historical value. In all of these cases the quest has been for freedom and dignity. One might assume that when these are obtained, the unifying myths will lose their magic, and peoples will take greater pride in their present accomplishments rather than in those of an often imaginary and utopian past.

THE CLASH OF MYTHS

As economic and political interests clash between newly awakened nationalisms, so also do the

113

memories and myths of history. Where geographical propinquity or intermingling of rival peoples exists, it is not strange, as nerve rubs against nerve, that this should be so, and that a people should emphasize those elements in its unifying myth which serve to counter and to belittle the pretensions of its rival. Mutual exacerbation heightens the intensity of commitment to myths that sadly and often tragically divide peoples of a common humanity and sometimes even of what one would imagine should be a common community. Perhaps the most dramatic and fateful arena of such clashes between myths is the contemporary Middle East. It is not strange that one of the side effects of the war of 1967 between the Arab states and Israel should be, as we have already seen, that in areas occupied by Israel, UNRWA should have difficulties with the history textbooks (as well as texts in other fields) which it had used to teach young Arab refugees. Today, as a result of Israeli protests over the contents of such texts, UNESCO has undertaken the task of rewriting acceptable books for these schools. One decision has been to substitute documents for some of the earlier discursive texts with the hope that students will then be encouraged to make up their own minds, and UNRWA can escape the accusation of pro-Arab prejudice.[94]

The Israelis argued that the Arab textbooks in use at UNRWA schools violated the Universal Declaration of the Rights of Man by preaching hatred, while Arab delegates argued that the schools in

[94] UNRWA-UNESCO, *op. cit.*

114

question were located in "occupied" land only, that they fell under the sovereignty of the several Arab countries involved, and that Arab governments had the right to teach their youth the history of the injustice that had been perpetrated against the Arabs with the creation of Israel. At one point, the minister of Education of Syria even said: "The hatred we instil in our children from birth is a sacred emotion." And, quoting from a textbook for six- and seven-year-olds, the Jewish delegate to UNESCO, Moshé Avidor, read the statements: "Jews are enemies of the Arabs," and "Jews are evil criminals." UNESCO finally resolved to appoint a committee of outside experts to study the textbooks in question, and this committee made the recommendations discussed elsewhere in this chapter.

There is, of course, much substance to the Arab's case against the historical claims of the Israelis. One statement of the Arab refutation of the Zionist claim that Palestine, promised to the Jews by God, had been their homeland for many generations, that they had been driven out by force and, today, had the right to return, is made by Constantine Zurayk, one of the most distinguished spokesmen of the Arab cause today.[95] His argument is that the Hebrews infiltrated into Palestine as other tribes had earlier; that their kingdom (1017-937 B.C.) included only a part of Palestine; that the kingdom split into two parts (until 722 B.C. for the north and 586 B.C.

[95] Constantine K. Zurayk, trans. R. Bayly Winder, *The Meaning of the Disaster (Ma'ana al-Nakbah, 1948)* (Beirut, 1956), pp. 60-62.

115

for the south); that they never again established a united state; and that, in any case, the plains and the coast were continuously dominated by the Philistines who, indicatively, were the ones to give their name to the area. In addition, Zurayk observes that the eastern European Jews are of Khazar and not of semitic stock (they embraced Judaism in the eighth century A.D.). In contrast, the Arabs who came in the seventh century A.D. were able to Arabize remnants of all previous peoples present, including those who had been in Palestine before the arrival of the Hebrews. The Jews, therefore, have no more claim to Palestine than the Arabs to Spain (which they ruled wholly or in part from the eighth century to 1492). Other points made by Zurayk are that Christians can hardly sanction a claim made by a people who have rejected the Christian message and who, in their Zionist form, are secularists in any case; their only justification for the seizure of Palestine can be that of force, not religion (which to secular Zionists is only a form of propaganda). Finally, Zurayk's argument is that the claim of the Zionist Jews to be the "chosen people" ends by resembling the pretension of the Nazis to be the *Herrenvolk.*

The Israeli myth, taught in both school and adult textbooks, is that Palestine, the "land of our ancestors," was first promised to the Hebrews by Jehovah, then by the British as a "national home" in 1917 (the Balfour Declaration), and, finally, was sanctioned by the United Nations in 1948 after it had already been in part bought from Arabs and in part developed out of nothing.[96] As for the areas occupied since 1967, according to Eric Rouleau,[97] terms like Judeah and Samaria are currently used to designate parts of Cis-Jordan in press and conversation, and the term "recuperated" or "liberated" are freely used to refer to what Mrs. Golda Meir in her investiture speech in March 1969 referred to as "our national patrimony," and General Dayan as areas "situated in the heart of Jewish history." Commenting unhappily on the new annexationist spirit in Israel, Hebrew University's Professor Talmon has stated that the conquest of the new territory seems to many Israelis to be "an ineluctable historical outcome."[98]

In franker moments, Zionists have conceded the justice of the Arab claims. Thus General Dayan has admitted that were he an Arab he would be a member of the *Fidayeen* (the Palestinian fighters for the liberation of Palestine from Zionism), and an eminent Israeli, General Y Harkabi, Israel's first direc

[96] Eric Rouleau, *Le Monde*, July 3, 1969.

[97] Ibid.

[98] The Jewish scholar Abraham J. Heschel was so excited by the Zionist victory of June 1967 that he claimed it to be evidence of Israel's revelatory role in the service of all mankind! He stated: "Suddenly we sensed the link between the Jews of this generation and the people of the time of the prophets . . . an eternal link. . . . We are God's stake in human history." (Quoted in *Time* March 14, 1969: 55-56.) For an excellent brief account of the crisis following the Six-Day War see Malcolm Kerr, *The Middle East Conflict*, October 1968, Foreign Policy Association Headline Series, No. 191.

tor-general of military intelligence, admits that "The Zionist claim to a 'historic right' sounds to the Arabs as if their own occupation of Palestine was morally deficient."[99] To conclude this discussion of the conflicting historical claims to Palestine of Jew and Arab, one might quote Colin Legum's perceptive comment: "Theirs [the Palestinians'] is not simply a refugee problem. It is the Jewish problem all over again: the problem of a people with a strong national consciousness who have been uprooted and alienated, and who demand a national homeland of their own within their historical territory—their Holy Land."[100]

[99] Quoted in Colin Legum, "The Wound and the Knife," *The Observer*, London, June 1, 1969: 8. For anti-Zionist interpretations of Zionist claims to Palestine see Jakob Petuchowski, *op. cit.*, and Hans Kohn, "Zion and the Jewish National Idea" in *Reflections on Modern History: The Historian and Human Responsibility* (Princeton, 1963), pp. 179-211.

[100] Colin Legum, *op. cit.* More broadly, Eric Rouleau, in a series of articles in *Le Monde*, July 2-6, 1969, entitled "Israel: le ghetto des vainqueurs," argues that Israel, a nation established to provide freedom and security for a disadvantaged minority, has turned into what, to the Arabs at least, is a case of unblushing Western colonialism in the midst of the Arab world, and an attempt to end the ghetto of the persecuted by creating "the ghetto of the victors." Rouleau quotes General Dayan as saying (July 3) that he realized Arabs hated the Israelis justly, from their point of view, "as Westerners, foreigners, invaders who have taken an Arab land to turn it into a Jewish state." The best critique of Israel from this point of view is Maxime Rodinson's *Israel et le Refus Arabe: 75 ans d'histoire* (Paris, 1968).

118

Another area of the clash of myths appears over the interpretation of the decline of Islam as an effective and united political power. In this case the rivals are the Arabs and the Turks. The Arab point of view has been that decline began around the middle of the thirteenth century, after Baghdad was conquered by the Mongols, and when the Turks, a people accused of introducing "despotic methods" by Arab apologists, became increasingly the dominant military element in the Muslim East.[101] This point of view, W. C. Smith observes,[102] leads some contemporary Arab historians to end their histories of Islam in 1258, with the fall of Baghdad, and so the end of the golden age of Islam. To the Turks, on the other hand, Islam thrived under their leadership which, among other things, brought a revival under the Seljuks (eleventh to fourteenth centuries); helped defeat the Crusaders; spread Islam to India (the Moghul dynasty); finally stopped the intrusions of the Mongols; destroyed and islamized the Byzantine empire (thus including eastern Europe in the Muslim sphere); produced the great mosques of Sinan; and made rich contributions to the Muslim mystical tradition (Sufism). It is understandable that a Turkish scholar like Halil Inalcik (Professor

[101] Laroui, *op. cit.*, pp. 22-24, is one of the more enlightened Arabs who criticizes his people for blaming all their troubles on the Turks. Contrast this with the spirit of a Khalid M. Khalid who sought to derive the word tyrant from the word "Turan." See *Muwatinun la Ra'aya* (*Citizens, not Subjects*) (Cairo, 1958), pp. 17-18.

[102] *Op. cit.*, pp. 164-65.

of Ottoman History at the University of Ankara) should cite as an example of "national prejudices" which often "overshadow historical realities" the case of a "well-known Muslim scholar" at a conference in London in 1950 who argued that the decline of Arabic literature was the result of Turkish domination over Muslim countries.[103]

Within the Arab world itself, clashes occur between defenders of the extended nationalism of the Pan-Arabists and the local nationalisms of the upholders of the "Berber myth" in Algeria, the advocates of the Egyptian myth of their descent from ancient Egyptian civilization (Pharaonism as it is sometimes called), and, within the small state of Lebanon (divided almost equally between Christians and Muslims), those who argue Lebanon's Phoenician descent and identity.

In the case of Algeria, a group of French officials (preeminent among them Camille Sabatier), following the principle of *divide ut imperes*, arranged to have special privileges given the Berbers in the late nineteenth century and sought to encourage cultural and legal differences between the Berber- and Arabic-speaking people of Algeria.[104] In its extreme form, proponents of the "Berber myth" went so far as to argue that the Berbers are descendants of the Vandals, and so Nordic; that they were Roman and Christian deep in their souls; that in contrast to the

[103] *Op. cit.*

[104] Charles-Robert Ageron, *Les Algériens musulmans et la France (1871-1919)*, 2 vols. (Paris, 1969), pp. 267-92, 873-90.

Arabs they were handworkers, democratic by inclination and institution (enjoying government by the *jama'a*, the assembly of elders); and that they, unlike the Arabs, could be easily assimilated into French culture. After Algerian independence, Robert Gauthier wrote an article on "Naissance et Mort du 'Mythe Kabyle' (de 1830 à 1914)" in which he warned that with the attainment of independence, destructive old historical wounds had been opened in the struggle for power that followed liberation and that one of these was the Berber-Arab division some Frenchmen had fostered.[105] And Abdallah Mazouni indicates, sadly, that "berberism" as a cultural political force is far from dead.[106]

In Lebanon, as one would expect, to the Muslim sector of the population the Phoenician theory is anathema because it claims for Lebanon a specificity (and therefore a sovereignty) which is non-Arab, except for language, and which is pre-Islamic. That many Muslim Lebanese not only resent what they claim to be their inferior status in Lebanon, but also strongly object to the Christian historical pretensions, can readily be seen in a pamphlet entitled *Moslem Lebanon Today*[107] published in Beirut in 1953 and endorsed by a host of prominent Sunnites and Shiites. Among the demands made are these:

Cessation of the printing, distribution, and use of textbooks for government schools which propa-

[105] *Le Monde*, October 9, 1963.
[106] *Op. cit.*, pp. 76-80.
[107] Use here has been made of the version translated into English.

121

gate Lebanese history and sociology from the exclusive viewpoint of one sect to the exclusion of equal prominence for Arabism and the viewpoints of the other groups and sects [Article 9]; cessation of specific attempts on the part of the Department of Tourism to present Lebanon to tourists as a Christian country and to suppress anything which indicates the presence of Islam in this country [Article 10]; extension of the scope of the National Museum to give equal prominence to Arabic and Moslem antiquities and art works of Lebanon instead of restricting its display to pre-Islamic pagan and Christian objects only [Article 11].

The argument is made that Lebanon was created by the Allied Powers (after World War I) without taking into account the views of a majority of the people who wanted a united Arab state; that the French, to rule more easily, created Lebanon artificially as a mixture of different sects; that among these sects they encouraged the preeminent rule of the Catholic Maronites; that Syria was truncated to make a "Greater Lebanon" in the same spirit; that the independent Lebanese government supports Christian but not Muslim education. The accusation is made that: "Under the Crusaders, who tried to impose their alien European state on this part of the Arab world, the Maronites served as a special corps of archers for the Franks against the Arabs and their Church entered into communion with Rome, spurning even Eastern Christianity." We have seen that Saladin is an outstanding symbolic hero; of him the writers of the pamphlet state:

> In meeting these threats [from the Maronites] we should take heart from the example of our great Saladin, Sultan of Islam, who, in spite of tremendous odds and the fact that the Crusaders had been established here for nearly a hundred years, was able to rally the Arab and Moslem peoples and to begin the freedom of our land from the earlier threat of subjugation to Europe. . . . And should God crown our struggle with victory, we must be equally prepared to follow the lesson of Saladin in justice, honor, toleration, and respect for our non-Moslem fellow citizens, guaranteeing to them those rights of religious freedom, toleration, and equality which they now deny us."[108]

But it is not only Lebanese Muslims who have challenged the Lebanese myth. Among Christians who have so done, each from a particular perspective, are Kamal Salibi, author of the best history of Lebanon to date and a devoted Lebanese nationalist, and the late Nabih Faris, an American citizen of Palestinian origin but a longtime resident of Lebanon as professor of Islamic history at the American University of Beirut, and a person who identified himself with the Arabist cause.[109] In a satirically

[108] For a brief treatment of the tensions between the two Lebanons see Abou, *op. cit.*, pp. 198-205.

[109] *The Modern History of Lebanon* (London, 1965). Dr. Salibi has indicated to the author that he is not happy

titled article, "Lebanon, Land of Light," Faris sought to refute the thesis of the Lebanese "who hold that present-day Lebanon is racially and culturally the direct heir of the Phoenician, Hellenistic and Roman heritage, and that its ties with the Arab world are therefore both tenuous and accidental, limited in the main to language."[110] And Faris disparaged Lebanon's claim to being the medium through which the West civilizes the East. Among his points are that none of the important Phoenician cities was in traditional Lebanon (Mount Lebanon) proper, in fact the Phoenicians were on bad terms with the mountain tribes; similarly, the important centers of Hellenistic culture were outside Lebanon; the famous Roman law school in Beirut was a foreign institution with Hellenized teachers; the Lebanese contribution to the period of flowering of Arabic-Islamic culture was minimal, the Lebanon (the Mountain) being a rather unruly and inaccessible haven for minorities; under the Ottomans Lebanon was virtually cut off from the outside world culturally; and it was only by chance that Lebanon made so important a contribution to the Arab Awakening of the nineteenth century, a "result of . . . rivalry between the foreign missionaries and their schools." In any case, Faris asserted, many of the leading

---

about the title of his book, one insisted upon by the publisher, because it suggests, contrary to Salibi's theme, that there was an "older" history of the "Lebanon" he discusses, a fact Salibi denies, as indicated in what follows.

[110] In Kritzeck and Bayly Winder, pp. 336-50.

figures of the *Nahda* found that they could do their best work in Egypt. Inevitably, and much to his consternation, this article aroused considerable indignation among some of Professor Faris' Christian colleagues. Rather touchingly, on the reprint he gave to the present writer he inscribed, "To Dave who will not doubt my loyalty to Lebanon and to truth."

Kamal Salibi, in contrast to Faris, has a reputation for being one of the most energetic defenders of Lebanese sovereignty, and he has been accused of rather negative views in regard to Arab nationalism and, unjustly, even to Islam. It was intellectual probity that led him to challenge the "Phoenician myth" in *L'Orient*, in an article entitled "L'Historiographie libanaise: histoire de vanité" ("Lebanese historiography, a history of vanity").[111] To the extent that this attack represented any ideological orientation, it was that of the more enlightened Christian Lebanese nationalist who realizes that Muslims must be encouraged to feel Lebanese and that Lebanon can only survive amid the Arab world by reasonable compromises with the Arab and Islamic elements outside and within Lebanon. In any case, Salibi's point is that Christian Lebanese historiography has exaggerated Lebanon's cultural role and has deformed history to suit its purposes—Lebanon does not need such vainglory to justify itself and to endure. Between Phoenicia and modern Lebanon, Salibi maintains, there is an unbridgeable gap. Except for the persistence of some names, the coiffure

[111] *L'Orient*, May 23, 1965.

called *labbadeh*, and a few popular terms, modern Lebanon has no relation to Phoenicia. In fact, until the early seventeenth century, Lebanon was culturally an integral part of Palestine and Syria, and only then, with the establishment of the Emirate, and later, at the hands of the Great Powers in the middle of the nineteenth century, did Lebanon assume a particular identity. The founder of Lebanon can be said to be the Emir Fakhreddine II, but even his Lebanon was limited to the "Mountain" only, and he and his successors were designated as "Emirs of the Druze," not of Lebanon. Here Salibi opts for the greater accuracy of the myth of the community of the Druze over that of the Christian, or of the Muslim who sees Lebanon's as only a part of Arab history in general. It is out of this original nucleus of Druze rule that the "Lebanon" that Salibi treats in his *Modern History of Lebanon* emerged.

Our final example here of a myth of a particular part of the Arab world that runs counter to the myth of a common and continuous Arab history since Muhammad is the case of what has been termed Pharaonism. This doctrine claims that Egypt has a pre-Islamic identity going back to the Pharaohs, and that it has a distinct personality that links it, some of its proponents would say, with the West rather than the East. Egyptian nationalism first emerged in the late nineteenth century with 'Urabi Pasha, the military commander whose uprising inspired the British occupation in 1881; was developed by 'Abd al-Nadim, a journalist, and Sa'ad Zaghlul, the ideological and political leader of Egyptian nationalism in the twenties; and was defended by the great literary figure Taha Husayn until the mid-forties,[112] when he argued that Egypt was essentially a part of Europe, a reality that had been obfuscated during the period of Turkish predominance. In more recent years, Husayn has moved toward Arab nationalism, and he has made considerable use of Muslim symbolism in his art—in his movie of the life of the Prophet, for example.

One of the leading opponents of Pharaonism among the prophets of Pan-Arabism has been Sati' al-Husri, who insisted that the basis of Arab nationalism was the Arabic language (he had read Fichte) and that Egypt was definitely a part of the Arab world and should, because of its large population and the cultural importance of Cairo, assume the leadership in the Pan-Arab cause.[113] Nevertheless, the Pharaonist impulse is still a factor in Egypt and more may be heard of it in the future. Indicatively, it was only two years after his assumption of power in 1952 that Nasser became converted to the idea that one of Egypt's historical roles was to assume the leadership of the Arab cause. Before this he had been, essentially, an Egyptian rather than an Arab nationalist.[114]

[112] Hourani, *op. cit.*, pp. 273-77 and chapter twelve.

[113] Ibid., pp. 311-312 and Haim, *op. cit.*, p. 42.

[114] See Gamal Abdul Nasser, *op. cit.* Nasser discusses (p. 3) the manner in which he and his colleagues, even in the heat of the Palestine conflict (1948), thought only of Egypt. But as he matured as a statesman, Nasser states, he came to realize Egypt's triple destiny, to serve as leader

127

The present discussion suggests that one man's myth is another man's poison—thus Pan-Arabism to many Christian Lebanese and to some Egyptians is a threat to their identity, while to Pan-Arabists the claims of some Lebanese to Phoenician identity and of some Egyptians to a Pharaonist specificity are aberrations, barriers to the coveted union of all Arab peoples. In the final analysis it is for men to decide which identity they prefer, unless, of course, they are constrained by superior power to do otherwise. But as seen in some of the cases considered, the sense of identity of a people can stubbornly persist under many overlays.

MYTHS AND UNIVERSALITY

The use and misuse of historical heroes and incidents as symbols, and of unifying myths to

---

of the Arab world, in the African world, and in the Islamic world. Of the three, it should be noted, he considered the first role the most crucial. According to Ibn El-Assal, *op. cit.*, pp. 78-81, the scene in Cairo has once again changed and many Egyptians now blame their troubles on Arabism and wish a return to Pharaonism. The Christian Copts, he observes, have always favored the latter. He considers it significant that *al-Ahram*, Egypt's most influential newspaper, published a discussion of the thesis of a Soviet scholar that the name Cairo is of pre-Arabic origin. In regard to Nasser's "Arabism," Miles Copeland, who was intimate with the Egyptian President in the earlier stages of the latter's accession to power, insists that the "conversion" to Arabism came at least two years after the revolution of 1952, and even then involved more the adoption of a tactical "myth" (to strengthen Egypt's international

combat the colonizer's historiographical pretensions and the myths of rivals, as well as to "reanimate" a people to a sense of its historical value through such media as historical textbooks, have produced much historical reconstruction that is fanciful and extravagant. But this tendency to historical reanimation appears to be a typical if not an essential feature of the struggle for decolonization. It appears to constitute a phase in the effort of a colonized and once passive people to return to the stage of historical action as participants—a sort of adolescence through which a colonized people must go before it can attain to a new phase of poise and self-confidence. It is a dangerous phase, however, and one which is divisive from the point of view of humanity as a whole, as well as from the point of view of existing structures, in the United States, for example, in respect to the extremist black separatists. Of course, the responsibility for this ethnocentric tendency lies more with the strong, who have or seem to have dominated and oppressed, than with the weak, who have been their victims. In the present context it is understandable, for example, that the overbearing myths of conquerors and colonizers should have evoked equally ethnocentric and proud myths from the conquered and colonized. The manufacture of the sometimes extravagant myths that have been discussed in the present chapter, and

---

influence) than devotion to Arab unity as an end in itself. See *The Game of Nations: the Amorality of Power Politics* (Birkenhead, 1969), pp. 56-57, 162-63, 168-69.

129

their clashes, are largely symptoms of a malaise which plagues beleaguered humanity in the twentieth century. But to the extent, limited as it may be, that historical symbols and myths are causes of the malaise, they should be submitted to the surgery of critical and scientific history whose methods and whose aspirations are, ideally, supranational and which assume, along with his specificity, the universality of man.

3

THE "COPERNICAN" REVOLUTION

THE TITLE of this chapter is taken from a phrase used by the Algerian historian Mohamed Chérif Sahli to suggest the need of a decolonized people to rewrite their own history from within, in terms of the colonized as subjects, rather than as objects, pawns in the game of the colonizers and their historians. The phrase might be taken to symbolize in exaggerated but dramatic form the impulse of the colonized to revise the history of their nation, to date written by professional historians and publicists from among the colonizers.[1] While this chapter deals with the "decolonization of history" of Algeria, in particular, and North Africa more generally, it might be pointed out that this impulse is widespread among the Third World, as it has been among oppressed peoples of the West, in the nineteenth century in particular.[2] For the Third World,

[1] Mohamed Chérif Sahli, *Décoloniser l'histoire* (Paris, 1965). See Jean Ziegler, *Jeune Afrique* September 25, 1966: 19, who asks quite seriously if one should not also "decolonize" sociology. In his research for the author in Tunisia, Rashad al-Imam found that all the educators he talked to—futurist as well as apologist—agreed with Sahli's call for radical revisionism.

[2] Revisionism of course is a constant characteristic of historiography, see Schlesinger, Jr., *op. cit.*, or Pieter Geyl, *op. cit.*, for example. And revisionism, in the West, can go to as absurd and anguished lengths as among newly inde-

133

however, in contrast to the West, revisionism has the particular characteristic of involving, to one degree or another, the ambivalent urge both for an authentic restitution of a non-Western past and for an effective entry into the modern world hitherto represented by the West.

The demand for revisionism—scientific as well as emotive—among the intellectuals of the Third World can be found in many shapes and forms. Thus, Nehru argues that the conventional chronological division of Indian history into Ancient or Hindu, Muslim, and then British is highly superficial because it deals with changes at the top only. It ignores, among other things, the rises and falls of the first period; the fact that the Muslims were culturally absorbed into what they had conquered; and the fact that the British were "outsiders, aliens, and misfits in India," that they did not touch the authentic continuum of Indian history.[3] Memmi, on a more theoretical level, argues that in the schools of the colonizer, the colonized is taught another's memory, not his own, which he needs to recover, and one

---

pendent nations of the Third World. One could point to the historiography of Nazism, or, today, of Communism with its perpetual rewriting of the history of World War II and of Stalin. A particularly rich discussion of communist revisionism appears in K. S. Karol, French edition, *La Chine de Mao* (Paris, 1966). A current joke goes: "What is the most difficult task for a Communist? Answer: To predict the past." This is quoted by Anatole Shub in *The International Herald Tribune*, March 28, 1969.

[3] *Op. cit.*, pp. 215-16.

of the major complaints of black Africans, as we
have seen, is that the Europeans have treated Africa
as if it were a continent with no history.[4] Pannikar,
in his estimable reconstruction of Asian history during the period of colonization,[5] tries to show that,
contrary to what many Westerners fondly imagine,
Asians studied Western methods not out of admiration but in order to find the sources of power with
which to defend their own identities. Particularly
sensitive to the need for a "Copernican Revolution,"
in Africa at least, is Thomas Hodgkin:

> Our profound ignorance of African history, our
> lack of comprehension of African attitudes to the
> contemporary situation, our remoteness from the
> ideas of revolutionary democracy, the distortions
> in thinking produced by our colonial mythology—
> these, I would suggest, are good reasons for doubt-
> ing whether we are likely to have any sensible
> contributions to make to a discussion of the di-
> rection of social and political change in post-co-
> lonial Africa. Such questions are best left to
> Africans.[6]

And a sympathetic Westerner, Jacques Berque,
observes that in North Africa, while the French saw
themselves as modernizers and benefactors, the
indigenous saw France as a destructive and alien

[4] *The Colonizer*, p. 104.

[5] K. M. Pannikar, *Asia and Western Dominance: A Survey of the Vasco da Gama Epoch of Asian History 1498-
1945* (New York, n.d.), pp. 316-17.

[6] Quoted in Apter, *op. cit.*, pp. viii-ix *n*.

deus ex machina in their midst, simply a new version of the eternal enemy, the new Rome and Byzantium.[7]

Both sides in the controversy mentioned by Berque are, of course, right. The debate may often seem futile to professional historians, but on a visceral level it is real and will so remain until the day when arrogance and a feeling of inadequacy give way to poise and common sense. But one particular difficulty of attaining such a stage of maturity in the case of the Third World is that its intellectuals sometimes tend to regard critical historiography, as first developed in the enemy West, as an aspect of colonialism rather than, as with the pure sciences, based upon a universal methodology. To the extent that Western historians have abused historiography to serve partisan ends, they are, of course, partly responsible for this suspicion. In any case, in the present chapter the discussion of the clashes of the myths of the colonialist and the counter-myths of the colonized is resumed but, here, not on the level of emotive myth-making, but on the level of historiography as practiced by professionals, popularizers, and pretenders. The focus will be upon French North Africa with particular reference to Morocco and Algeria.

REVISIONISM IN NORTH AFRICA

By way of introducing the historiographical debates in contemporary North Africa, seven of the basic issues of interpretation over which bitterness,

[7] *French North Africa*, pp. 98-99.

accusation, and counter-accusation have been excited on the professional, middlebrow, and journalistic levels will be considered.[8] That some of these seven issues are raised at all, certainly in the passionate manner they have been, points to the fact that during the experiences of colonialism and of contemporary decolonization historiography is as much visceral as it is mental. These debates are as much grist for the student of decolonization, in

[8] For discussions of the debate see John Wansbrough, "The Decolonization of North African History," *Journal of African History* 1968 (IX:4): 645-50; Ernest Gellner, "The Struggle for Morocco's Past," *The Middle East Journal* Winter, 1961: 79-90, and David C. Gordon, *The Passing of French Algeria*, pp. 183-90. For an account of tensions over historical interpretation partly motivated by patriotic considerations, on a highly professional level, see *Le Monde*, December 8-9, 1969. At the Second International Conference of North African Studies, at Aix-en-Provence, Abd El-Kader Zghal was attacked for the role he assigned to Moroccan tribalism in the development of the nation. To some of his compatriots his theme seemed too reminiscent of certain colonialist themes. Bruno Etienne, in turn, was attacked for contrasting legal façade and the social political reality of struggle for power in North Africa. Perhaps this is the place to make clear that almost all of the countries discussed in the present book can boast of historians who would meet any professional standard anywhere. They are not discussed particularly in the present work because they largely transcend the mythologies under discussion. Among such historians one would surely rank, for example, Abdul-Aziz Duri, an eminent Iraqi historian of the Abbasid period, Constantine Zurayk, and Nabih Faris. Among the up-and-coming young Tunisian professionals would be included Mohammed Talbi, author of *L'Émirat aghlabide (184/800-296/909): histoire politique* (Paris, 1966).

137

other words, as for the professional historian. Just as the recourse to "counter-myths" has been felt necessary in order to challenge the myths of the colonizer, so, in the present context, does the sort of revisionism outlined below appear to be part of a necessary stage before a people can attain to the universal. But the relative academic rawness that often characterizes the stance of revisionists among the historians of new nations, as well as of their colonialist counterparts, does not preclude the possibility that as a result of their debates windows to the past will be opened and fresh hypotheses be advanced.

In each case below the thesis of a composite stereotypic colonialist is followed by its rebuttal at the hands of an equally stereotypic composite of the views of North African nationalists and their leftist sympathizers in France.

1. The colonialist historian has maintained that because of its geography—the inaccessibility of some areas like the Atlas Mountains, Kabylia, the Sahara, and the easy accessibility of the coastal area—North Africa has been destined to disunity and to foreign conquest.[9]

[9] C. A. Julien, as rewritten by Christian Courtois, *Histoire de l'Afrique du Nord*, I (Paris, 1956), pp. 12, 14, 16, 48, talks of the importance of the geographical factor in North African history. For example, the steppe "plays the premordial role in the human evolution of North Africa." And: "The parceling into autonomous compartments has compromised political unity but favored, in Kabylia and in the Aurès, for example, the formation of original groupings which to this day have resisted the erosion of history."

138

This thesis has been countered with the observation that if this geographical determinism were so, any conquering foreign power ruling North Africa likewise would rapidly disintegrate. Moreover, it is false because Berbers and Arabs were united in North Africa in the twelfth century under the Almohads. The reason for the foreign conquests of North Africa was the superiority in power of the conquerors, not any geographical predetermination. To the extent that French historians argue or imply that geography is a determining rather than only a conditioning factor, the "Copernicans" are, of course, justified in their indignation.

This first dispute merges into and is complemented by the second:

2. The colonialist has sometimes maintained that the stock people of North Africa, the Berbers, have been in character changeless over the centuries, tribalistic and unstable, with no talent for cooperation and organization; that they have been incapable of founding any state that has lasted long (each of their states has represented only the interests of a clan, soon overthrown by other clans). The Berbers have, therefore, been destined to be conquered by others, and the history of North Africa is as a result the story of alien domination, by the Phoenicians, the Romans, the Byzantines, the Arabs, the Turks, and, finally, the French.[10]

[10] Mostefa Lacheraf, *L'Algérie: nation et société* (Paris, 1965), p. 15, rejects the thesis propounded by Malek Bennabi and, in a different way, by Albert Memmi, that North Africa was colonized because it was "colonizable." Lacheraf

This position is countered with the observation that viable states have been formed (e.g. the Hafsids of Tunisia, thirteenth to sixteenth centuries; the Almoravids, eleventh century; and the Almohads, twelfth century), and that it is unhistorical to see the Berbers as unchanging—that efforts to establish states under unusual leaders such as Jugurtha (died 104 B.C.) and Massinisa (died 149 B.C.) often succumbed only to superior force.[11] In any case, neither the Phoenicians nor the Arabs were conquerors in any ordinary sense because, racially and culturally akin to the Berbers, they were relatively easily admitted and integrated into the Berber world, as were the Berbers into theirs. This latter argument, parenthetically, is a case of *post hoc ergo propter hoc*, and would have applied as much to the French as to the Phoenicians and Arabs had the

---

belongs among those decolonizing historians who believe that without colonization their country would probably have made more progress than it did under colonialism.

[11] Sahli, *Décoloniser*, p. 18, quotes Julien-Courtois, *op. cit.*, as suggesting that North Africa appears to be congenitally incapable of maintaining its independence. But Sahli, and herein lies the irresponsibility of some of his polemic, fails to observe that the text also states that there is no reason to suppose that but for considerations of power Massinisa and others might not have established native states. Courtois, in fact, rejects the notion of the Berbers' innate incapacity as a colonialist ruse and he points out that similar clichés about Turks, Russian peasants, and the Chinese have been disproved. Relatively little is known about the Berbers, Courtois concludes, pp. 28-29.

French remained longer in North Africa or had the younger Ferhat Abbas won his case for assimilation.

3. With all their weaknesses, colonialist historians have said, the Berbers worked out a nice balance between sedentary and nomadic life before the middle of the eleventh century when the Fatimids, for purposes of vengeance against the client Zirids, released the hordes of the Banu Hilal and others upon North Africa. These wild, anarchic Beduin Arabs destroyed and undermined all in their path, upset the balance, reduced the area of sedentary agrarian life, and created such disruption that chaos ensued. These Arabs and those nomadic Berbers like them (the Zenata) are the destroyers, in contrast to the well-behaved sedentary folk (the present Berber-speaking Kabyles in Algeria, for example, who have preserved their own culture and with whom the French can and should work).

The replies to this argument are various: one is to question the size of the nomadic wave; another is to argue that the decadence that finally made way for the Turks was caused by the drying-up of the gold routes to Africa, not by these Arab Beduins who were often the allies of different dynasts and useful as protectors of caravans.[12] Understandably, a deep

---

[12] The Lacoste argument is that the shift in gold routes (to favor Mamluks, Genoese, and Portuguese, the latter after 1450) increased poverty and led rulers to become more exploitative and so added to political instability. It might be observed that French historians cited by revisionists such as Sahli also question pet colonialist themes.

141

resentment is felt against those French who have pictured Arab and Berber as different in quality and nature, as eternally hostile; all this in the interest of dividing to rule.

4. The French have said the Turks were an alien people who ruled in North Africa as conquerors. They were exploitative and their only "industry" was piracy.[13] Their state included only parts of Algeria. The French in 1830, thus, simply replaced an alien regime; they did not conquer a "nation" that did not exist, or even an Arab state.

Among the answers given in rebuttal to this disparaging picture of pre-French Algeria is that Algeria was recognized by other states with whom commercial treaties were signed and that while its Turkish government might not have been popular, it was Muslim and so could evoke an allegiance the

---

Thus, Georges Marçais is cited in *Décolonisation* against the Hilali catastrophic theory, as is Fernand Braudel in his monumental *La Méditerranée et le monde méditerranenée à l'époque de Philippe II*. See Sahli, *op. cit.*, pp. 65, 81, 85-86. In regard to the perpetual enmity of Berber and Arab, the revisionists have an ally in Nevill Barbour, *Morocco* (London, 1965), pp. 175-76, who dismisses the notion as untenable and suspect of ideological motivation.

[13] The view of Algeria as purely a "piratical" state is challenged in Fernand Braudel, *op. cit.*, and in Godfrey Fisher, *Barbary Legend. War, Trade and Piracy in North Africa* (London, 1957). Both authors maintain that regular trade was a most important part of Turkish Algerian life and that piracy was by no means a monopoly of Algeria before the nineteenth century. Almost all Mediterranean powers indulged in it.

Christian French could not. It is also argued, but this remains a matter requiring a great deal of fresh research, that the Algerian state was much more developed economically than it has been portrayed as having been and that its schools enrolled more children, proportionally, than did France's at the time of the conquest. But this dispute slips into the fifth.[14]

5. According to the French, the Amir Abdelkader who led a popular resistance movement against the French from 1832 to 1847 was a "fanatic" Muslim who represented only part of Algeria, certainly no Algerian "nation." The Kabyles rejected him, and he had to fight constantly against religious lodges rival to his own.

Here, the decolonizers are especially sensitive. Abdelkader is their hero, as we have seen, and the more extravagant of them see him as the first hero of an Algerian "nation" to resist France, a resistance

[14] Lacheraf, *op. cit.*, p. 44. But Algerians have also argued the contrary theory out of patriotic impulse, namely, that the Turks were exploiters and unlike Abdelkader had no real contact with the masses. See Gordon, *The Passing of French Algeria*, p. 186. In regard to the issue of the Turks in Algeria, a book written well after independence reveals how unreconstructed "colonialist" myths can persist. Marcel Peyrouton, the veteran diplomat, in his *Histoire générale du Maghreb: Algérie-Maroc-Tunisie: des origines à nos jours* (Paris, 1966), pp. 133-34, states that the Turks who exploited North Africa "*sans mesure*" and made piracy and slavery their "national industry," provoked "sanctions too long delayed," and prepared the way for the arrival of the Europeans.

that continued until final victory in 1962.[15] They see him as a person who tried to lay the basis for a genuinely Arab Algerian state, and even as something of a "modernizer."[16]

Algerian nationalists are as sensitive to the French claims that after his defeat in 1847 Abdelkader became a friend of France as they are to the charge of Abdelkader's alleged "fanaticism." Sahli, thus, goes to great pains to try to disprove that Abdelkader discouraged the revolt of 1871 against the French and that he took pride in honors bestowed upon him by Napoleon III.[17] The propagandistic myth of Abdelkader's alleged change of heart in regard to France was based in large part, argues Sahli, upon forged documents (letters purportedly from Abdelkader to his son Mohyeddin discouraging his involvement in Moqrani's revolt in 1871, for example).

6. The Algerian Revolution, and the Tunisian and Moroccan nationalistic movements, the relatively

[15] The Moroccan political leader and ideological "apologist" sees the resistance to the French imposition this way. 'Alal al-Fasi, trans. Hazem Nuseibeh, *The Independence Movements in Arab North Africa* (Washington, D.C., 1954), pp. 9-10. Sahli, one of the leading protagonists of the present chapter, is the author of a laudatory life of Abdelkader, *Abdelkader le chevalier de la foi* (Algiers, 1953).

[16] For a penetrating study of Abdelkader's ideology see Pessah Shinar, " 'Abd al-Qādir and 'Abd al-Krīm: Religious Influences on their Thought and Action," *Asian and African Studies* (Israel), vol. I (1965): 139-74.

[17] Sahli, *Décoloniser*, pp. 27-57.

liberal colonialist would have it, resulted from France's failure to provide enough reforms, to assimilate to full equality, for example, those Muslims of the elite without demanding they give up their Muslim status, as had been proposed for Algeria during the years 1936 to 1939, in vain, in the famous Blum-Viollette Bill.[18]

The answer is that this is sentimental nonsense; the North Africans would never have accepted assimilation, and independence would have come, sooner or later but inevitably. This debate is a matter of conjecture on both sides, involving one of the "ifs" of history, but it is a debate over which much passion and energy are expended.

7. Finally, the colonialist maintains that France created the possibility of Tunisian, Moroccan, and Algerian unity by providing the infrastructure, and the necessary mobility, without which a "nation" in any modern sense is impossible.

While some North African nationalists would admit this, although insisting that it was in the dialectical nature of capitalistic imperialism, others, Algerians in particular, insist that there were always "nations," in one sense or another, in North Africa, and that the most the French did was to weaken or suppress elements of Muslim and Arab culture, exploit the masses, cut the elite off from them, and leave them in a state of abysmal ignorance and pov-

[18] In the author's *The Passing of French Algeria*, pp. 34-48, the thesis is argued that the Blum-Viollette Bill could at best have only postponed the struggle for independence.

erty.[19] In a sense, this debate involves arguments that are at cross-purposes and a matter of semantics. While the one side claims to have made a "modern" and united Algeria possible, for example, the other side argues that there was always a "nation" even if it lacked modernity and unity. Some of the heat could be taken out of the debate if the term "nation" were used less passionately and defined more precisely.

These seven areas are among the major ones in which intellectuals like Mohamed Lahbabi and Abdelaziz Benabdellah of Morocco, Paul Sebag and Salah-Eddine Tlatli of Tunisia, and Mohamed Sahli and Mostefa Lacheraf of Algeria, with their French Marxist allies like Yves Lacoste, have challenged the classical interpretations of French historians. Several other related areas of historiographical dispute will be considered as our discussion proceeds.

THE CASE OF MOROCCO

Some of the classical French themes, argued on a scholarly level and representing what revisionists

[19] According to Lacheraf, *op. cit.*, p. 24, when the French landed in Algeria in 1830 "France found before her a well-organized society, with its own civilization, not very different from the other societies of the Mediterranean basin, perhaps imperfect in its development, but one whose love of liberty, attachment to the land, cohesion, culture, sense of patriotism, resources, and common ideals she would defend against the national enemy, as she proved during the course of a war of conquest that lasted almost forty years."

claim is the French colonialist point of view, appear in what has been considered the standard general history of Morocco, Henri Terrasse's *Histoire du Maroc*, published in Casablanca, in 1940 and 1950.[20] Moroccan critics of Terrasse appreciate his scholarship and his sympathy for the Moroccan peoples; they do, however, question some of his basic assumptions and theories.

One of Terrasse's underlying themes is that Moroccan society has been essentially tribalistic, that the prime loyalties have been biological rather than territorial, to a real or imagined ancestry, and that because of this it has been impossible for Moroccans to establish a nation in the Western sense. Unity has only been temporary; the only serious movement of unification, the Kharidjite (puritanical) movement of the eighth century, and the resistance to Christian Spain and Portugal (fifteenth through sixteenth centuries) were essentially negative. To unite, wrote Terrasse, "il fallut presque toujours une volonté étrangère ou, à tout le moins, un adjuvant extérieur" (Rome, for example).[21] With Islam, the authority of the Caliph, absolute in theory, was in fact limited by the supremacy of the law—whose defender, not whose interpreter, he was—and his efficacy by the fact that no adequate principle of succession was worked out. Sooner or later, the

[20] *Histoire du Maroc: des origines à l'établissement du protectorat français*, 2 vols. (Casablanca, 1949-1950). A shortened English version is Hilary Tee, trans., *History of Morocco* (Casablanca, 1952).

[21] Ibid., p. 410.

147

tribalistic spirit of the Berbers prevailed, and the ideal of the Berber confederation frustrated the ideal of the Muslim emirate. The Almoravids, the Almohads, and the Merinids (eleventh through fifteenth centuries) were dynasties each of which, in effect, represented the domination of one or another Berber confederation. The ideal of a *"patrie marocaine"* was never fulfilled.[22] By the end of the fifteenth century, the division of Morocco into the *bled al-makhzen*, the area effectively controlled by the Caliph (Sultan), and the *bled al-siba*, the less accessible areas where traditional Berber life continued and the Caliph, though enjoying religious respect, had no real administrative authority, had become a permanent feature of Moroccan social and political life. The Morocco upon which the French imposed their protectorate in 1912 and whose effective conquest by the French and Spanish was completed by 1934 is characterized by Terrasse in the following way: "In this country, abandoned [*livré*] to the particularism of the tribes, to the egoism and the cupidity of the chiefs, the notion of the common good was unable to develop and devotion to the public good was hardly more than a matter of individual virtue."[23] All efforts at unity were always brought to nought by a "native indiscipline, an invincible penchant to anarchy."[24] This was essentially the same condition that led Ibn Khaldun in the fourteenth century pessimistically to settle for a cyclical theory of history. In the sphere of culture, in spite of thirteen centuries of Islam,

[22] Ibid., p. 414.   [23] Ibid., p. 422.   [24] Ibid., p. 444.

no unity was realized: "Agrarian animism, magical rites were preserved. . . ."[25]

But with the French, and after 1934, the *bled al-makhzen* was able to extend its control and authority, as it had never been able to before, over all of Morocco, and orthodox Islam could extend itself at the expense of local cultural forms. France thus deserves credit for uniting Morocco as well as opening her up to the outer world from which she had for centuries withdrawn. But this very success, Terrasse feared, had its dangers. Open to the Arab world as well as to the West, Morocco was now, several years before independence in 1956, becoming infested with the "xenophobic demagoguery" of Pan-Arabism which could only bring Berbery "new spiritual troubles . . . political agitation."[26] This, in turn, threatened the local "democratic" customs dear to Terrasse, and opened the Berbers to "agitation and misery" instead of the order they enjoyed within the French empire.

Ernest Gellner[27] has already discussed with perception and insight the two strains of nationalistic Moroccan revisionism to the approach to Moroccan history represented by Terrasse: the apologetic and the futurist. By coincidence, a representative work of each trend was published in the same year, 1958, two years after independence. These works are Abdelaziz Benabdellah's *Les Grands Courants de la civilisation du Maghreb*, introduced by the leading

[25] Ibid., p. 441. [26] Ibid., p. 467.
[27] Gellner, *op. cit.* The following discussion parallels and echoes Gellner's article.

Moroccan political figure and apologist 'Alal al-Fasi, and Mohamed Lahbabi's *Le Gouvernement marocain à l'aube du XXe siècle*, introduced by a man already discussed as a leading futurist, Mehdi Ben Barka.[28]

As Gellner observes, Benabdellah, *qua* historian, is old fashioned, his method is one of "scissors and paste," while Lahbabi is critical and analytical. The former simply seeks to refute the "French myth" by citing the glories of Morocco's past and trying to show that Islam is the most tolerant and wise of all religions. Lahbabi, on the other hand, while using his analysis of what he considers to have been the real nature of the Caliphate in the past, seeks to confound not only the past French administration of the Protectorate, but also to attack, by implication, what to him (and Ben Barka) is the presumption of the present monarchy to absolutism. Benabdellah speaks with uncritical enthusiasm of Morocco's traditional past; Lahbabi indicates that while more rational than the French historians have indicated, the Moroccan administrative set-up was archaic in many respects and inadequate for the purpose of genuine social and economic reform.

In regard to Terrasse's synthesis, Benabdellah makes the following points in attempted refutation: the sedentary Moroccan peasantry did have a sense of territorial loyalty (symbolized by the *agadir*, the wheat silo owned in common to serve in hard times) like all peasants everywhere; and they did have a sense of a "national consciousness, almost a Moroc-

[28] Lahbabi, *op. cit.* Abdelaziz Benabdellah, *Les Grands Courants de la civilisation du Maghreb* (Casablanca, 1958).

can patriotism" as evidenced by the common resistance to the Christians (during the fifteenth and
sixteenth centuries). But here Benabdellah ignores
Terrasse's point that this resistance was essentially
negative, although real. Terrasse, Benabdellah continues, is unfair in belittling the greatness and the
accomplishments of the Almoravid and Almohad
empires, and irresponsible in failing to indicate how
much Alaouite caliphs like Moulay Ismail did do for
their people. Other points in rebuttal include the
statements that Terrasse exaggerates the Roman im-
print (terms of Roman origin used by Berber peasants, Benabdellah says, come from the Andalusian
and not the Roman period), and that Terrasse is
wrong in suggesting Christian sources for Kharidjite
purism. Finally, Benabdellah argues, Terrasse fails
to point up adequately how seriously the European
powers took Morocco as a sovereign state in the
sixteenth century and after, witness the many commercial treaties between them and Morocco.

Lahbabi does not address himself to Terrasse's
synthesis in particular but by implication his whole
book is a refutation of the idea promoted by the
French administration, and, although in a qualified
form, accepted by Terrasse: that the Caliph-Sultan,
having absolute power, could delegate to French administrators the power they needed to rule absolutely. Lahbabi's thesis is that the Caliph's authority
in Morocco was always limited and only delegated
power, that through the ceremony of investiture
(the *bay'a*) local elders delegated this authority
when they chose to and withheld it when they did

151

not wish to delegate it. This limitation upon the Sultan's authority rested upon both Islamic principles and upon Moroccan tradition. In the nineteenth century Morocco was a member in the concert of nations, an "independent state, highly individualized."[29] The French Protectorate power ignored this individuality of Morocco, as we have seen, and the present monarch, in ruling arbitrarily, is perpetuating the perversion of Morocco's historical "constitution."

The import of Lahbabi's historical reconstruction is at least threefold. First, it implies that it is false to argue as Western historians have that Morocco was not a viable or complete state because it allowed for a vast region of self-administration. Further, the French perverted the Moroccan system by assuming falsely that the Sultan was an absolute ruler and could therefore grant absolute power to French administrators. And, finally, the King of Morocco today is unjustified in behaving as if he had absolute power. The intent implicit in Lahbabi and explicit in Ben Barka is that Morocco has a historical basis for democracy, although by no means should one return to the particular forms of this historical past, which were obviously inadequate for the establishment of a progressive, secular, democratic nation.

THE CASE OF ALGERIA

In contrast to Morocco, a protectorate at least in theory and only ruled by the French from 1912 to 1956 (and in the north by the Spanish), Algeria

[29] Lahbabi, *op. cit.*, p. 194.

was dominated from 1830 to 1962; it had been administratively absorbed into France from 1848, and was dominated culturally as well as politically and socially by a large *colon* population of about one million by the eve of the Algerian Revolution. One could further add to this brief contrast that the Moroccans had successfully resisted Ottoman domination while Algeria had been ruled by the Turks from the sixteenth century until the French conquest. Not strangely, therefore, Algeria's quest for identity and for reestablishing its link with its past has been that much more difficult and, for this reason perhaps, historical revisionism among its intellectuals has been that much more extreme than has been the case with Morocco and, certainly, with Tunisia.[30]

Until about 1929 the historiography of Algeria was almost completely dominated by French scholars and publicists, and the turning-point, not surprisingly, came with the emergence of the first Algerian political and cultural nationalistic movements. The debate in Algeria can be divided into three stages which overlap but which, roughly, follow one another chronologically. The first was Islamic in inspiration, the second was liberal and humanistic, and the third has been secular, nationalistic, and Marxist.

The first revisionist attack on French historiography of Algeria, starting about 1929, came from the pens of members of the Association of the Reform-

[30] See Brown, *Tunisia, the Politics of Modernization.*

153

ist *'Ulema,* the movement which at this time sought the return of Islam to its past purity, the extension of the Arabic language, and, although it was discreet politically, Algerian cultural independence.[31] The motto of the Association was: "Islam is my religion, Arabic is my language, Algeria is my fatherland." At this time, most of the French-educated Muslim elite, while wishing to keep their Muslim identity (symbolized by Muslim law in respect to marriage and inheritance), were assimilationist. They wanted reforms which would provide Algerian Muslims with full access to French citizenship without asking them to abandon their legal status as Muslims. This was the position of their outstanding spokesman, Ferhat Abbas, who could inspire the wrath of the leader of the Association, Sheikh Ben Badis, by declaring that there had never been an Algerian nation, that the future of Algerians lay with France.[32]

[31] Saadeddine Bencheneb, "Quelques historiens arabes modernes de l'Algérie," *Revue Africaine* (Algiers), vol. C (1956): 475-99.

[32] The debate between Abbas and Ben Badis is frequently referred to in contemporary histories of Algeria. In *Entente*, February, 1936, Abbas stated that no *"patrie algérienne"* existed, that he had been unable to find one although he had looked for it even in "the cemeteries." Because one could not "build on the wind," he concluded, Algeria's future lay with France. Ben Badis, in *Ech-Chihab* (*The Meteor*), April, 1936, claimed that he could find an Algerian nation both in the past and in the present, that this nation possessed its own language and religion, and had a glorious history. This nation neither wanted to become part of France, he asserted, nor could it become so even if it so wished. For Abbas' *mea culpa* for his assimilationist days see his *La Nuit coloniale,* I (Paris, 1962). This book is,

Although the first historical works in modern Algeria appeared between 1900 and 1910—Abu al-Qasim al-Hafnawi being the most notable of the early historians—they were medieval in spirit, uncritical, mixing legend and fact. It was not until 1929 and 1930 that a modern approach appeared when Al Mubarak al-Mili (1880-1945) published the two volumes of his *Tarikh al-Jaza'ir fi-l-qadim wa-l-hadith* (*History of Algeria in the Past and in the Present*) in Constantine, a study covering the period from prehistoric times to the sixteenth century. The importance of the historical quest he described thus:

History is the mirror of the past and the ladder by which one rises to the present. It is the proof of the existence of peoples, the book in which their power is written, the place for the resurrection of consciousness, the way to their union, the springboard for their progress. When members of a nation study their history, when the young get to know its cycles, they know their own reality, and so insatiably greedy nationalities in their neighborhood do not absorb their nationality. They understand the glory of their past and the nobility of their ancestors and accept neither the depreciations of depreciators, nor the discrediting of falsifiers, nor the lies of the prejudiced.[33]

Al-Mili denounced both miraculous historical legends which encouraged the people to rely on the

---

as one might expect, revisionist, but it relies almost exclusively on French sources.

[33] Quoted in Bencheneb, *op. cit.*, pp. 480-81.

155

supercelestial rather than upon themselves and French colonialist historians who saw a Roman lurking in every Berber (the novelist Louis Bertrand came especially under attack). Al-Mili made use of French authorities like Gautier and Gsell in translated form, and his method consisted rather too much of piling quotation upon quotation from secondary sources. Nevertheless, his material was well-organized and relatively critical.

More impressive was Ahmed Tewfik al-Madani (born in 1899 in Tunis), a person educated in both French and Arabic culture and a leading figure in Algeria during the Revolution and for a period after it. His intent was similar to al-Mili's: to show Algerian Muslims they had a history and so a nation. In his *Tarikh shamal Iffriqiyya aw Qartajinna fi arb'a usur* (*History of North Africa, or Carthage over Four Centuries*, Tunis, 1927), the Carthaginians are seen as civilizers and not, like the Romans, conquerors. Racially and culturally they were akin to the Berbers, in contrast to the Romans; the same was true of the Arabs, also brothers and not conquerors in any ordinary sense. In 1932 al-Madani published *Kitab al-Jaza'ir* (*History of Algeria*, Algiers) in which he denounced the possibility of the assimilation of Algeria to France and with the use of statistics, many drawn from Maurice Viollette's *L'Algérie vivra-t-elle?* (Paris, 1931), he denounced French colonial rule.[34] A third historian of the period

[34] These same themes are found in Laroussi Khelifa, *Manuel du militant algérien*, I (Lausanne, 1962), and in Amar Ouzegane, *op. cit.*

was 'Abd al-Rahman, b. Muhammad al-Jilali, author of *Tarikh al-Jaza'ir al'am* (*General History of Algeria*, Algiers, 1954, vol. I). Joseph Desparmet, an Arabist and a keen follower of cultural trends in Algeria (in the pages of *L'Afrique Française* and other French colonialist journals), saw these histories as significant not for any scientific content they might have, but because of their inspirational and nationalistic intent, and he suggested that these historians, so dangerous to the French presence, were giving a systematic form to the ideas and assumptions of popular oral folklore.[35]

The second period involves the attack on colonialist historians by liberal-minded French historians like Charles André Julien who sought to point out the great in North Africa's past and the iniquities of colonial rule. Their assumption was similar to Abbas', namely, that Algeria with reform and benign and intelligent handling could be made genuinely a part of France. Most members of this group changed, when the Revolution broke out, to favor negotiations with the Algerian rebels and then even independence (but hopefully with close links to France). The historiographical stance of these "liberals" was perhaps most forcefully stated by Marcel Émerit in an article written on the eve of the outbreak of the Algerian Revolution. In it he analyzed Algeria in 1830, contrary to the official French view, as rich in educational facilities and possessing, as shown by their resistance under Abdelkader, "a great moral

[35] See in particular "Naissance d'une histoire 'nationale' de l'Algérie," *L'Afrique française* 1933: 387-92.

energy."[36] Anticipating Sahli's notion of a "Copernican Revolution," he stated: "The history of Algeria since 1830 has been based, almost exclusively, on French documents and studied from a European point of view [*dans un esprit d'Européen*]. In this country, no attempt has been made to understand the Muslim soul."[37]

The third period involves the attack upon French historiography by French-educated nationalists writing in French and their radical Marxist allies in France (Yves Lacoste and the like). Now the attack is upon even the liberal-minded French like Julien who, to the assimilationist elite of the thirties and forties (the Abbas type), were inspirations. Sahli refers to the classical French historians of North Africa as "*cette Pléiade d'auteurs*" who more or less deliberately, he maintains, in spite of their valuable scientific contributions, sought to demoralize the indigenous and to justify the colonial regime.[38] The "hotbed" of these "colonialist" historians, and other professors, was the University of Algiers. The list of those attacked include E. F. Gautier, Georges Marçais, Christian Courtois, Léon Gauthier, Henri Pérès, Gabriel Camps, Henri Basset, Roger Le Tourneau, Stéphane Gsell, Gaston Bou-

[36] "L'État intellectuel et moral de l'Algérie en 1830," *Revue d'Histoire Moderne et Contemporaine* April-December, 1954: 119-212.

[37] C. A. Julien feels that Emerit, in this article, exaggerates the amount of education available in Algiers before 1830 out of reaction to colonialist historians. See *Histoire de l'Algérie contemporaine*, p. 520.

[38] *Décoloniser*, pp. 11-12.

thoul, Pierre Boyer, Jean Lassus, and Julien himself. These constitute a mixed bag ideologically, but Lacheraf does not discriminate when he says of their approach that it was *"tour à tour cynique, insidieuse, débonnaire, perfide, paternaliste et faussement objective."*[39] In criticism of their research Sahli makes the point that they deliberately neglected the archaeology of the Berbers because of their ideological preference for things Roman (in digs they sacrificed Berber remains in the process) and their interest in things Arab-Muslim was negligible.[40] Lacheraf adds the accusation that after the Revolution Algerian historians were denied their own documents by "tons of tons" when the French government exported all the official documents they could to France.[41] To Lacheraf this was a "gigantic material rape aiming to dry up or to deroute the vital sources of this history [of the modern Algerians]."

This revisionism among Algerians thus includes the traditionalists of the reformist 'Ulema and the more recent French-trained nationalists whose work is more sophisticated and less apologetic in tone. Both groups agree that French historiographers have abused the history of their past to justify French colonial rule (as heir to Rome), to divide Berber and Arab, to demoralize the indigenous in terms of confidence in their past and so their future, to belittle any hope for creating a "nation" that never was and so never could be. In this resentment they were joined by allies from outside of history proper like

[39] *Op. cit.*, p. 42.
[41] *Op. cit.*, pp. 42-43.
[40] Sahli, *Décoloniser*, p. 138.

Frantz Fanon who implored the Algerians, and the inhabitants of the Third World generally, to reject, with violence, the colonizer and reenter their own reinvigorated history as participants rather than as shadows in the drama of the colonized. To date the leading Algerian decolonizers have been Mostepha Lacheraf, one of the leaders of the Revolution, and the French-trained historian Mohamed C. Sahli. The two outstanding books which revise Algerian history from the French Marxist/anti-colonialist point of view are *L'Algérie Passé et Present* (Paris, 1960) by Yves Lacoste, André Nouschi, and André Prenant, and Lacoste's polemic *Ibn Khaldun, Naissance de l'Histoire* (Paris, 1969), an attempt to refute what he considers the perverse misuse of the main source for much of medieval North African history by colonialist historians.[42]

These men are the attackers; to evaluate what they have to say it might be helpful to look at two representative figures among the attacked, in order to observe more closely the nature of this impassioned revisionism. Selected for brief discussion are one of the outstanding figures of the group of geographer-historians who taught at the University of Algiers, and while contributing seriously to the knowledge of North African history was a clear apologist of French colonial rule, E. F. Gautier, and,

[42] Lacoste, Nouschi, Prenant, *L'Algérie, passé et present: le cadre et les étapes de la constitution de l'Algérie actuelle* (Paris, 1960), with a preface by Jean Dresch; Lacoste, *Ibn Khaldun: naissance de l'histoire passé du tiers-monde* (Paris, 1966).

with him, one of the most liberal-minded critics of colonial abuses, a friend of the native Muslim, Charles André Julien, once critic of the Gautiers, now subject to "decolonization."

How unapologetic a colonialist Gautier (1864-1940) was can be seen in a small book he wrote for the extravagant celebrations of the centenary of 1930. In this work, entitled *L'Évolution de l'Algérie de 1830 à 1930* (Algiers, 1931), Gautier baldly praised France's role in Algeria as having brought prosperity to a land impoverished since the days of France's anticipator, Rome. The participation of Algerians in World War I proved, he wrote, their identification with France which had offered them an "ideal," while their previous conquerors, Arabs and Turks, had brought only exploitation and poverty. "The hypothesis of Algerian independence," he declared, "is inconceivable."[43]

Gautier wrote, it should be noted, when the influence of the *Nahda* (the Arab cultural and national renaissance) had begun to make serious inroads into the body of Algerian Islam. Algerian nationalism had already manifested itself in the form of the Paris-centered North African Star founded in 1925, and in 1931, the year Gautier's volume was published, Sheikh Ben Badis founded the Association of the Reformist *'Ulema*.

[43] Gordon, *The Passing of French Algeria*, pp. 19-20. Perhaps Gautier deserves some credit for proposing a statue of Abdelkader to be placed next to one of General Bugeaud in central Algiers. The *colons* laughed him out of court.

161

But Gautier, besides being an apologist for French Algeria, was also a prolific and inventive scholar (even his critics admit that he threw out many valuable hypotheses). His most important book (1937), the leading *bête noire* of the revisionists, in the present context, is his *Le Passé de l'Afrique du Nord: Les siècles obscurs*, first published in 1927 under the title *L'Islamisation de l'Afrique du Nord.*[44] In it, relying heavily on Ibn Khaldun's *Prolegomena*, he sought to uncover the principal lines of historical development during the least familiar period of North African history, between what he called the two Arab "invasions," at the end of the seventh century and by the Hilali and Sulaym tribes in the middle of the eleventh century.

Writers as sympathetic to Islam and the indigenous peoples of North Africa as Julien and Jacques Berque have praised the *Siècles obscurs* for its seminal ideas but have certainly expressed serious reservations about many of its theses.[45] To the impassioned nationalist revisionists this book is the very model of colonialist arrogance and the most important single effort, perhaps, to demoralize Arabs and Berbers in regard to their history. North Africa was seen by Gautier as inhabited by a people con-

[44] The edition used here is the pocket one (Payot), new ed., Paris, 1952.

[45] *French North Africa*, pp. 373-74, and C. A. Julien, rewritten by Christian Courtois, *Histoire de l'Afrique du Nord: Tunisie-Algérie-Maroc des origines à la conquête arabe (647 ap. J.-C.)* (Paris, 1956), describes the work as full of "ingenious and fecund ideas even if they are not always right" p. 295.

162

genitally unable to unite or form a state, always subject to foreign domination. The sedentary Berbers are good; the Beduin Arabs who cataclysmically invaded in the eleventh century were "black angels of destruction," who began a period of decline leading to the Turkish conquest. Neither good Berbers nor bad Arabs had any sense of a state or a nation and their only identification was a biological (*contra* a territorial) one with imaginary clan ancestors. This in oversimplified form is the message revisionists see in the book. Its implication is that only a power like France could bring unity and prosperity to such a people, in such a region of the globe, as Rome once had. The tenor of Gautier's analysis might be suggested by this excerpt:

> Instability is not the particular characteristic of our man but of his race and society in which he lives. In Berbery, and elsewhere throughout Islam, fidelity is something eternally incomprehensible. . . . When the Romans accused the Carthaginians of being unable to trust one another they were right. If one attempted to characterize the psychology of the Oriental . . . one would probably find that the most striking fact is the absence of any emotional [*sentimentale*] base upon which to erect national solidarity. One might admit that there is here an incurable individualistic imperfection [*tare*]. Today, still, Berber individualism, the eternal principle of instability, is an element with which one must reckon, by way of guarding against it and by way of making use of it.[46]

[46] Gautier, *op. cit.*, p. 81.

How the revisionists would answer Gautier in general has already been suggested. More particularly, Lacheraf in *L'Algérie nation et société* argues that many of the ills, the lack of a creative bourgeoisie, for example, that Gautier uses as arguments for Algeria's backwardness were the product of colonialism. Thus, for example, the undermining of artisan industry because of French industrial competition caused many members of the middle class to sink into the proletariat. Gautier, according to Lacheraf, in fact projects into the past the ills of today, ills for which France is responsible. Sahli argues that Gautier's contrast of the good sedentary and the bad nomad is artificial and pernicious. The two groups, most of the time, cooperated with the nomads serving the producers as traders and mercenaries. As for Yves Lacoste, he rejected the whole cataclysmic Hilali theory as based upon a misreading of Ibn Khaldun.[47] The arrival of the Hilali, in

[47] Lacoste, *Ibn Khaldun*, pp. 94-95. Ibn Khaldun has, of course, usually been a source of great national pride to the Arabs, but it is interesting to note that on occasion some of his conclusions about North African Muslim civilization have been considered dangerously unflattering. In a work on Arab nationalism, *Al-Qawmiyya al-arabiyya* (Cairo, 1960), Ahmed Fuad al-Ahwani saw Ibn Khaldun as having been taken up by colonialist historians because of his attacks on "Arabism" and, for a period, Ibn Khaldun's works were once banned in Iraq for this same reason. See *The Times Literary Supplement* August 8, 1968: 853. See also Lacoste, Prenant, Nouschi, *op. cit.*, pp. 71-72. Gautier is here described as the leading colonialist falsifier of history, as in Lacoste, *Ibn Khaldun*, p. 87.

fact, is seen by Lacoste as more of an invitation than an invasion. And Lacoste joins Sahli and Lacheraf in seeing the view of the congenitally tribalistic and incompetent Berber as well as the image of the destructive Arab as racist and a device to justify French rule.

The second author under discussion, Charles André Julien, professor of history at the Sorbonne, would agree with some of these criticisms of Gautier. His *L'Histoire de l'Afrique du Nord*, significantly, was published at the same time as Gautier's centenary bit of propaganda, in 1931.[10] To Muslim Algerians, as well as North Africans generally, it came as an inspiration and a more than welcome refutation of much of the boasting of the centenary and the belittlement of North Africa's past. Mahmoud Bouayed, director of the National Library of Algiers, testifies to this.[49] He says that to young Muslims like himself Julien was a tonic of hope: North African history was treated with respect, its great accomplishments described, Berbers and Arabs were treated as human beings like others—the

[48] Note that Julien's *Histoire* of 1931 should not be confused with the rewritten *Histoire de l'Afrique du Nord*, 2 vols. (Paris, 1956), which, although attributed to him, and which he prefaced, is a quite new work written by Christian Courtois (vol. I) and Roger Le Tourneau (vol. II). In his preface to Courtois-Le Tourneau, Julien indicates several points upon which he disagrees with his rewriters.

[49] Mahmoud Bouayed in *Revue Algérienne des Sciences Juridiques Politiques et Economiques* no. 3, September, 1966: 639-44.

Gautiers had been answered. The book, he states, was the *"livre de chevet"* to the young people of his generation.

Julien first arrived in Algeria (Oran) in 1906 at the age of fifteen.[50] Initially he shared the common racist prejudices of the *colon* youths with whom he became friendly. He remembers their thinking it quite normal fun to push Arabs off the sidewalks into the gutter. While at *lycée*, however, he changed. He befriended the only Arab present at his school (a person who later, because of racist prejudices, had great difficulty in pursuing his medical education). He became a defender of the native Algerians, perhaps, he speculates, because as a Protestant he belonged to a minority that had often been persecuted in past French history, perhaps because of his father who was a fervent Dreyfusard, or perhaps because of his great admiration for Jaurès. During the years 1911 to 1915 he began his career as a writer with two articles attacking the *Code de L'Indigénat* (which provided a special list of crimes for which natives could be punished). To this day he has considered himself a friend of the North Africans, first as a reformist and then as a sympathetizer with the various nationalistic movements. In the days of the Popular Front he served as a high official on Blum's High Mediterranean Committee and he strongly urged Blum to impose the Blum-Viollette Bill by edict if necessary.

On the eve of the Algerian Revolution he gave his compatriots more than ample warning—in his

[50] *Revue Africaine* February 20, 1965: 20-21.

L'Afrique du Nord en marche (1953)—of the storm they had carelessly and irresponsibly awakened. He observed that the abandonment of the Blum-Viollette Bill had brought the *évolués* close to nationalism and that the *"colons* had closed the way to the gradual integration of the indigenous into French citizenship. They had thus made the bed of nationalism that was now to rise with a new force."[51]

During the Revolution, in many articles and through petitions he signed, Julien stood against the use of torture and in favor of negotiations with the FLN that would lead to independence but in close cooperation with France. In 1964 he published the first volume of his splendid *L'Histoire de l'Algérie contemporaine* (*1827-1871*), which Roger Le Tourneau had accused with some justice of anachronistically recounting history from the perspective of the contemporary Algerian nationalist.[52] Why should such a man, Julien himself once wryly asked, now be on the list of the historians to be "decolonized"?

[51] *Op. cit.*, pp. 127 and 138.

[52] Roger Le Tourneau, *Annuaire de l'Afrique du Nord* (Paris, 1965) III: 1964, pp. 730-33. Le Tourneau, the late Robert Gauthier once observed to the present author, coming from a strong Catholic and military background, was never able to share the sympathy for Arab nationalism to which Julien, of a liberal and Protestant background, could be won over. Gauthier pointed out how little there is in Le Tourneau's otherwise estimable work, *Évolution politique de l'Afrique du Nord musulmane: 1920-1961* (Paris, 1962), about the more reprehensible methods of the French army that Julien so often denounced.

The Sahlis and Lacherafs do pay tribute to his greater "objectivity" as compared to the Gautiers, and Julien receives occasional praise from them as, for example, when he insisted that Adbelkader was a patriot and not a fanatic, and that his generous actions in Damascus in 1860 when he protected Christians during the massacres were the result of humanitarianism rather than any French patriotism.[53] But Julien is accused of treating the conquest of Algiers as something of an accident rather than a long-planned French venture,[54] and, more seriously, for denying the existence, in 1830, of something "analogous to the idea of a nation," not very different from eighteenth-century France. This alone, Julien's critics maintain, could explain the fierce resistance of Abdelkader and others up to 1871.[55] (On this point the Algerian nationalists and their Marxist French allies fall out because the latter indicate that in their opinion it was French colonialism, which they otherwise roundly denounce, that prepared the way, economically in particular, for the emergence of an Algerian "nation."[56] Julien is

[53] Sahli, *Décoloniser*, p. 50. But Sahli does criticize Julien for taking seriously "forged" documents purporting to prove that Abdelkader opposed the uprising of 1871.

[54] Ibid., pp. 88-92.   [55] Lacheraf, *op. cit.*, pp. 9-10.

[56] Sahli, pp. 128-32. The revisionism of Sahli and Lacheraf is also partly directed against Algerian conservatives who, today, defend a conservative present as the resurrection of a "nation" conquered in 1830. In regard to the Revolution and its antecedents, Lacheraf and Sahli also emphasize the crucial importance of peasant as opposed to bourgois resistance to France.

168

also accused of showing some sympathy for Napoleon III because of the latter's futile attempts to curb the voracity for land of the *colons*, and because of his respect for the enlightened administration of some of the military *bureaux arabes*. In more distant times, they observe, Julien accepts the "false" Hilali cataclysmic theory, and in more recent times, as has been seen, Julien believed, incorrectly according to them, that integration with France might have been possible had the Blum-Viollette Bill been adopted. Thus, Lacheraf rejects the whole interpretation of the failure of France in Algeria as a question of *"occasions perdues,"* because, in essence, the "system" was neither just, perfectible, nor viable.[57]

Julien is hardly the man to take much of this criticism lying down. He has replied in at least one introduction to a book and in several letters to *Le Monde* and *Jeune Afrique*.[58] Generally he has

[57] Lacheraf, *op. cit.*, p. 42; Sahli, *Décoloniser*, pp. 100-101.

[58] Pierre Nora, *Les Français d'Algérie* (Paris, 1961) and *Le Monde* February 15, 1961, and March 1, 1961, are among such examples. The *Le Monde* articles deal principally with the leftist polemic of Michel Habart, *Histoire d'un parjure* (Paris, 1961), a work which made extravagant claims regarding the population of Algeria in 1830, which it placed at ten million! This work's main thesis was that Algiers was conquered through perfidy—the Algerians were told that if they surrendered their religion and freedom would be respected. One source made use of by Habart was Sidi Hamdan Ben Khodja's contemporary work *The Mirror* which Julien dismissed as written for polemic reasons by Desjobert, a contemporary anti-colonialist, to discredit the French conquest and that, in any case, Habart

insisted that falsifying history can only be a dis-service to the young and the future by feeding il-lusions. Furthermore, he has refused to follow popu-lar currents and abandon historical objectivity: "In praising Ismail Urbain and in recognizing the merit of Napoleon III one is in a stronger position to con-demn Bugeaud and Warnier,"[59] he has said. He has refused to see Abdelkader as a "nationalist" repre-senting all the Algerian people (he was opposed by other lodges, by the city of Constantine, and by the Kabyles), but he has seen him as a great man with administrative ability and the desire to create a kingdom based on Muslim justice. And Julien has strongly attacked the scholarship of some of his critics like Michel Habart, and Sahli himself, who once, as his student, expressed such gratitude but now was subjecting him to "decolonization." In re-gard to Sahli, Julien has pointed out that on at least one occasion Sahli had given the opposite sense to Julien's text by quoting out of context.[60] As for his own liberal assimilationism in the days of the Popu-lar Front, Julien has admitted that he and his like had been over-optimistic and had underestimated the depth of the Arab and Islamic impulses among the Algerian masses. Today he has accepted inde-

---

had abused the use of this work by erroneously having its author refer to an Algerian *"patrie."* Serious historians generally take Habart's work for a rather irresponsible political tract, not on the same level with the Lacoste-type revisionists.

[59] Introduction to Pierre Nora, *op. cit.*, p. 10.
[60] Letter to the editor, *Jeune Afrique*, January 30, 1966.

170

pendence but has refused to sacrifice his scientific
values in order to avoid being called a "neo-colonialist," as once he had refused the same compromise
in order to evade the epithet "traitor" once hurled at
him by the colons. He would agree with Roger
Paret's suggestion that it is as absurd to argue that
because Algeria is a nation in the 1960s and 1970s
it must have been one in 1830 as to argue, as colonialist historians have, that because it was not a
nation in 1830 it cannot be one today.[61]

Finally, in his self-defense, Julien has pointed to
the fact that tributes to his friendship for North
Africa have been bestowed upon him in the past by
Muhammad V of Morocco and Bourguiba of Tunisia. But these are figures whose ideologies many
of the radicals of North Africa would also like to
"decolonize," to one extent or another. In the eyes
of the enemies of "neo-colonialism," a Gautier can
be dismissed as a reactionary whose theses the Revolution has already repudiated, but a Julien is still a
force for maintaining close links with France, with
the France that gave of her best to Algeria after
independence and continued to do so under the
regime of the man who has been, since independence, perhaps the most popular single figure in
North Africa, General de Gaulle.[62]

A crucial question that needs to be answered is
whether the conflicts in which a Julien has become

[61] Roger Paret, *op. cit.*, pp. 68-69.

[62] De Gaulle's creative policies in regard to Algerian independence, and to independent Algeria, are one of the
main themes in Gordon, *The Passing of French Algeria.*

involved are purely a matter of culture politics or whether the revisionism of the Marxist and of the Algerian nationalists has some historiographical justification. In regard to the Gautiers much of it has, of course, but so far as concerns the Juliens it is often unfair and, on a personal and professional level, offensive. But it has opened windows and raised questions that deserve serious investigation—for example, the importance of the withering of the gold trade through North Africa in the late Middle Ages and the nature and real significance of the so-called "cataclysm" of the migration of the Hilali and other tribes in the mid-eleventh century. And one might admit, as Julien has of himself, that many French scholars (mainly because they are not able to handle the Arabic language) tend to write about the French in North Africa rather than about the natives of North Africa. There is a place for what has been grandiloquently called a "Copernican Revolution" that will involve, *inter alia*, a greater use of Arabic and Turkish sources in the archives of Algiers and Istanbul as well as those in the palace archives in Rabat, and, to the extent that they exist, oral traditions. With this "revolution" scholars will penetrate more deeply than has been so far done into the social and psychological realities of the indigenous. In the case of Algeria since the conquest in 1830, however, Roger Paret observes how few are the usable Arabic sources the scholar has at his disposal. He suggests, pertinently, that this fact itself is an indication of the degree to which the colonizers in Algeria have "dehistorized" the colonized,[63] a situation, of course, which presents a problem for "Copernican" historians in many other ex-colonies also.

On a more general level, one might suggest that one of the tests of the success and reality of self-determination is the ability to consider one's own history objectively and openly. Tunisia, as suggested earlier, has attained, to a degree, this self-confidence, both in its espousal of bilingualism and in its self-conception of partaking in Mediterranean rather than purely Arabic culture, thus being able, unselfconsciously, to accept the culture of Paris as well as Mecca. Algerians, however, are still too confused about their identity, still too bitter with the memories of the Revolution whose psychic wounds have not yet healed, to be able, in many cases, to take Julien for the fine historian he is—publicly, that is, if not privately—or to profit from what is reasonable and suggestive in a Gautier.[64]

[63] There is thus something to Bouayed's thesis, *op. cit.*, that "the soul of the country is absent from the work." The work referred to is the *Histoire de l'Algérie contemporaine*. The same point is made by Marc Ferro, *L'Express* June 18-24, 1965, and by Paret, ibid., pp. 78-79. The present author concurs with this view. The book, brilliant as it is, treats of French Algeria rather than of the history of Algeria proper.

[64] See the author's *The Passing of French Algeria* and Henri Sanson, "Les Motivations de la personnalité algérienne en ce temps de décolonisation" in Charles Debbasch *et al.*, *Mutations culturelles et coopération au Maghreb* (Paris, 1969), pp. 6-16. Sanson remarks on the way many Algerians are today caught between the Scylla of passivity

Nevertheless, in spite of the self-conscious and propagandistic nature of their polemics, the Sahlis and Lacherafs, along with the Lacostes, of course, are raising questions whose stimulus to professional historiography may prove to be of considerable significance, particularly in opening the way to the study of the indigenous North Africans for themselves rather than as only part of the scenery of France *outre-mer*. But however useful the decolonizers have been in challenging old assumptions, ultimately, of course, serious critical history must transcend the apologetic and polemic spirit of the colonialist and the decolonizer alike.

(in seeing their identity in a now moribund past) and the Charybdis of an opportunistic, futuristic revery (as to the ease of modernization). Also of interest, here, is Assia Djebar's review of Mostefa Lacheraf's *L'Algérie: nation et société* in which she sees Algeria as floating between an "imported" culture she needs, and a "falsified, corrupted, disfigured" culture in which her people feel so deeply rooted (*Jeune Afrique* January 16, 1966: 30.)

174

CONCLUSION

HISTORY, SELF-DETERMINA-
TION, AND MATURITY

IN THIS final chapter consideration is given to several questions this study has suggested. Does history need to be true? That is, does it matter whether the past from which a people draws inspiration should correspond to any verifiable or probable past reality? Second, if the answer is yes, is it possible to know the past objectively or is man, by his very nature, bound to read it subjectively or mythically, in any case? Third, if some approximation to past reality is possible as well as desirable, is the attitude toward the past—the past taught to schoolchildren and propagated in mass media—a test of the relative "maturity" of a people, and if so is there a dialectic, a set of stages, along which a people seeking self-determination can be said to attain to such maturity, as judged by their view of their own past? These questions have been asked over the centuries, and many different answers have been given to them. Here, possible answers are considered in terms of what has preceded in this study and in the context of contemporary decolonization.

In his essay on "Lebanon, Land of Light" discussed earlier (above, p. 102n), Professor Nabih Faris shocked some of his Christian Lebanese colleagues by making light of some of the cherished myths of this small republic. One colleague wondered, petulantly, whether such myths, the life-force of a people according to him, could be submitted to critical examination with impunity. Should sleeping gods, so to speak, not be left undisturbed? Others have taken the less extreme position that historical myths can be excused as at least temporary measures to give a people, in sore need of it, a sense of pride and of cohesion. Thus, Bernard Lewis begs some indulgence for the Turanian myths of the Turks, and Thomas Hodgkin defends the use of crude methods of cultural propaganda in countries like Ghana as a way "of restoring the confidence of Africans in their capacity for political action; in their power, if they so choose, to affect the course of history."[1] Ronald Segal, in his passionate *The Race War*, defends the extravagant claims to the inventive originality of Africans—depicted in public murals in Ghana—as showing "how deep has been the hurt" and as an understandable attempt to regain self-confidence.[2] And Laroui observes, defensively, that such myths as an idealized democratic Athens or French Revolution have played a creative role in Western history.[3]

However sympathetic one might be to such appeals for indulgence, it is clearly dangerous to accept myths which feed *hubris*, which assume racial superiority, and which create barriers between members of the human race. Warnings to this effect have come from many pens in recent times: Raymond Aron sees the abuse of history by contemporary

[1] *Nationalism*, p. 168.
[2] *The Race War* (Boston, 1967), p. 7.
[3] *Op. cit.*, p. 102.

ideologists as the major excuse today for intolerance and crime;[4] Paul Valéry, in a frequently quoted statement, wrote:

History is the most dangerous product evolved from the chemistry of the intellect. Its properties are well known. It causes dreams, it intoxicates whole peoples, gives them false memories, quickens their reflexes, keeps their old wounds open, torments them in their repose, leads them into delusions either of grandeur or persecution, and makes nations bitter, arrogant, insufferable, and vain.[5]

And Nietzsche, in *The Use and the Abuse of History*, had already seen what he called "monumental" history as a weapon against the present, the inspirer of rashness and fanaticism.[6]

In regard to the Third World, in recent times in particular many warnings have been given about the dangers of mythical history on the grounds that one cannot reconstruct the national personality if one cheats with the past.[7] Perhaps one of the most fervent expressions of this concern appears in Emmanuel Mounier's *"Lettre à un ami africain."*[8] Mounier was for a long time an inspiration to Afri-

[4] *Polémiques* (Paris, 1955), p. 168.

[5] *History and Politics* (New York, 1962), p. 114.

[6] Adrian Collins, trans., *The Use and Abuse of History* (Cambridge, Mass., 1957), pp. 12-16.

[7] "L'Opium du passé" in Jean Lacouture and Jean Baumier, *Le Poids de tiers monde: un milliard d'hommes* (Paris, 1962), pp. 227-40.

[8] *Deuxième conférence*, I, pp. 37-43.

can intellectuals; his sympathy for their cause could not be disputed, so the more telling were his question whether African intellectuals were not "opposing a black counter-racism to white racism" and his warning against rejecting the West from which Africans had much to learn. Similarly, Fred M. Hechinger, in an article on "Black Separation in the Universities," suggests: " 'The black is beautiful' approach, in history as elsewhere, is an absurdity comparable to, say, the 'white man's burden' concept, but it is of little help in the task of weaving an honest, nonracist pattern of history, research and teaching."[9] And Jean Chesneaux and Axelos Abderrahim ask if the cult of the past does not keep alive institutions such as tribalism incompatible with modernity, and lead to the self-defeating rejection of the "colonial period" as worthy of an objective evaluation.[10] Even Frantz Fanon, in *The Wretched of the Earth*, sees the emphasis on the unique (be it racial or cultural) only as a means toward the attainment of dignity in universality and sterile as an end in itself. And another hero of decolonization, Taha Huseyn, has always insisted that the ability to criticize oneself is the mark of maturity and freedom.

One might conclude this brief discussion of the importance of historical veracity with the following wise, if obvious, statement of Daniel Boorstin:

. . . the study of history we conduct in a non-homogenized and very particular way has a positive

[9] *The International Herald Tribune*, January 22, 1969.
[10] *Op. cit.*

180

effect in enabling one to relive an experience of a person in many respects very different from us, and this in itself provides a positive good in learning about the nature of man. History provides a way of living through other lives than our own. It is used by way of amplifying experience, but it is only useful if it is a valid experience that is really happening.[11]

Related to the question of historical veracity is the question, which Nietzsche also treated with acumen in his *The Use and Abuse of History*, whether history, as a cult, might not inhibit progressive action and growth among a people. The tendency to live and breathe intellectually in the ambiance of an idealized past is particularly true among those intellectuals we have designated as "apologists." It is not only Westerners like W. C. Smith[12] who have observed that such a cult can be emotionally and psychologically disruptive, that it can inhibit a realistic approach to the problem of the present; this same observation is made by a number of Arab intellectuals, among others Nabih Faris, who saw his fellow Arabs as particularly prone to such a cult of the past.[13] Others would include the Moroccan Abdallah Laroui.[14] Malek Bennabi, who fervently denounces Arab apologetics as the reflection of an inferiority complex revealing the "quasi-infantile

[11] Daniel Boorstin, R. McCutcheon, *The Present Day Relevance of Eighteenth-Century Thought* (Washington, D.C., n.d., report of a conference held in 1956), p. 51.

[12] *Op. cit.*, pp. 87, 116.

[13] "The Arabs and their History."

[14] *Op. cit.*, pp. 73-92 in particular.

pathology of the Muslim world,"[15] and Constantine Zurayk, who explains the defeat of the Arabs by the Zionists as the result of the fact that the latter "live in the present and for the future while we continue to dream the dreams of the past and to stupefy ourselves with its fading glory."[16]

But granting the need for a true rather than an idealized and falsified vision of one's past, one might, with reference to the present period of historical decolonization, raise again the question whether objective history is possible, whether history is not inevitably a reconstruction of the past on the basis of conscious or unconscious assumptions or even faiths about the nature of man and of his destiny. This very question was discussed in a most suggestive manner at a conference a few years ago on "Historians of the Middle East," a discussion which engaged the talents of W. C. Smith, Albert Hourani, and G. E. von Grunebaum.[17] What is of particular interest in the present context about this debate is that it revolved around an assertion, made by von Grunebaum, that implied the cultural superiority in regard to historical understanding of the Western World over other civilizations, the Islamic

[15] *Op. cit.*, p. 18.

[16] Zurayk, *The Meaning of the Disaster*, p. 2.

[17] Albert Hourani, "General Themes: Introductory Remarks," pp. 451-56; G. E. von Grunebaum, "Self-Image and Approach to History," pp. 457-83; and Wilfred C. Smith, "The Historical Development in Islam of the Concept of Islam as an Historical Development," pp. 484-502. All these appear in Bernard Lewis, P. M. Holt, eds., *Historians of the Middle East* (London, 1962).

in particular. Smith, albeit in quite different terms, seemed to imply a similar superiority of Christianity over Islam on a religious plane. Hourani might be considered in this debate to be the spokesman, if not for a part of the Third World under criticism, at least for a type of ecumenical humanism.

Assuming that complete historical objectivity is impossible, that every people view history from the perspective of their own "self-image" (that is in terms of the aspiration of a society and in terms of its general philosophical view of the universe), von Grunebaum boldly asserts:

> The need to substantiate one's self-view through history, to find the justification of one's future in the past, is almost universal. But the needs of various self-views and aspirations of the future differ in the stylization they impose on known facts and the stimulus they give to the unearthing of hitherto unknown ones. Western research of the last generations has been fortunate in the co-incidence of its driving motivations, first and fore-most the will to self-understanding by means of understanding 'all' cultural solutions to the prob-lem of living, with the demands of factuality it-self. For the universal shades are only pushed away from the blood, they are not eliminated as shades.[18]

And further: ". . . one may speak of the superior attitude of the modern West for the analysis of civi-lizations. One may go further and describe it as the

[18] von Grunebaum, *op. cit.*, pp. 457-58.

183

only civilization that has, in its concept of man, utilized his *Kulturenfähigkeit*, i.e. his potential (and largely actualized) cultural pluralism."[19] In contrast, Arab historiography suffers from an almost exclusive self-concern, crude psychological interpretation, and the lack of the Greek-rooted tradition of "humanism." Arab historians, with several exceptions whom von Grunebaum cites, suffer in short from solipsism, defensiveness, and apologia. In his discussion of the concept of Islam in history, Smith virtually recommends that by way of "reformation" Islam shed much of its inherited baggage and emphasize its mystical and transcendant aspects, on a parallel with the Christian Reformation.

Answering von Grunebaum's rather arrogantly expressed opinions and those Smith stated more humbly, but which were nonetheless ethnocentric in implication, Albert Hourani questioned the extent to which the humanistic and pluralistic approach was as common to the West as von Grunebaum made out, and he observed that much of Western historiography is inspired by the "self-images" of purely Western motive forces, those of Marxism and Christianity, for example. He also raised the questions whether a creative historian need be circumscribed by his "self-image" to the extent von Grunebaum implied, and whether a historian with a limited and even prejudiced "self-image" might

[19] Ibid., p. 466. The claim for the West's unique contribution to historical consciousness and ecumenicalism is also made by Christopher Dawson, *op. cit.*, and by Hans Kohn in *Reflections on Modern History*, pp. 4-5.

184

not, by being true to the facts of course, produce creative and seminal history. In this respect he cited the case of Henri Lammens who, perhaps partly because of his anti-Muslim and "Arab" prejudices, made important breakthroughs in the study of early Islam.[20] Hourani pertinently asked if Smith was not asking Islam to become something other than what it was, other than a religion whose minimal characteristics were the Koran and the Prophet as well as man and God.

In regard to the issues raised in this debate, the writer's own position, as must have become apparent to the reader, is close to that of von Grunebaum, and his "self-image" is the "self-image" that von Grunebaum attributes to the West, but one trusts it is free of the rather arrogant and exclusive pride from which von Grunebaum's very learned article suffers. The Western approach to history of which von Grunebaum speaks is now universal—as is apparent in the growing number of historians of the caliber of Dike, Pannikar, Zurayk, and others whose orientations are humanistic and ecumenical. But it is not true of many of the more narrowly nationalistic historians and publicists considered in the preceding pages. It seems apparent, in any case, that in a period of decolonization and self-determination a people must go through the stage of myth-making

[20] Kamal Salibi, "Islam and Syria in the Writings of Henri Lammens," in Lewis, Holt, eds., *Historians of the Middle East*, pp. 330-42; Albert Hourani, "Islam and the Philosophers of History," *Middle Eastern Studies* January, 1967: 206-68, pp. 222-23.

and ethnocentric self-absorption. The hope is that this stage is a temporary one toward greater maturity which, in the author's own "self-image," means modernism and ecumenicalism.

Inevitably in a study like this one many terms have been used—"self-determination," "identity," and so forth—which are subject to philosophical questioning. The assumption has been made that their usage corresponds to reality as the reader also sees it, with no further ado. This assumption, rash as it may be for many of the terms used with little effort at elaborate definition, is certainly so of the concept "maturity." This concept has, in effect, been used throughout the present study as it is described, if not defined, in Karl Deutsch's *Nationalism and Social Communication*.[21] Deutsch draws the analogy between a national community and a ship tacking against the wind. In the first tack the national community, in a process of self-determination, needs to discover cohesion, to force its various parts into an effective whole. Diversity and localism must be combatted and transcended, and foreign influences eliminated. The state isolates the community, more or less, and seeks to admit only those technological

[21] pp. 57-58. Deutsch doubts if any nation to date has attained to the maturity of the "second tack." Perhaps it is relevant to quote, in this context, the answer made to Malraux by a priest who had heard the confessions of countless victims of World War II to the question as to what he had learned about man from this experience. The priest concluded his answer: "Et puis, le fond du tout, c'est qu'il n'y a pas de grandes personnes. . . ."

186

influences which can help it to catch up with and possibly surpass other powers. The community develops its own school system and its own mass communications until it feels the national culture "has been revived and established." Ultimately, this tack reaches its limit when it is felt that other powers are refractory to absorption into the national culture and when the sterility of a purely ethnocentric "stereotyped, repetitive, coercive power" is realized. The need now arises for a second tack. The community must now listen more and "broadcast less," it must open itself to foreign ideas and ways "without losing [its] own identity." It needs new values and strengths in addition to those it now has in order to grow. For this second tack, the community must be "well enough established to transcend lingering feelings of insecurity and fear, and their over-compensation by nationalistic bravado," and it must have institutions that are flexible enough to allow for change and adjustment. In this state of "maturity" the community will be characterized by a sense of hospitality, a tolerance, and enough resources to permit effective sharing of opportunities among its people. The extent to which a people approximate Deutsch's second tack, that is, "maturity," can be tested in various ways. One way, the one proposed here, is by its attitude toward its own past, its ability to see this past critically and even to indulge in fruitful debunking, or to treat the past with a sense of humor as in *1066 and All That* or *Astérix le Gaulois*.

A useful way of thinking about the process of

187

maturing in regard to historiography is in terms of stages toward full self-consciousness and universality. One possible stage-model suggested by the various experiences of decolonization that have been discussed is the following—the four stages outlined, if not ordered chronologically, are related to one another dialectically.[22]

In the first stage, the colonized is passive and accepts his inferiority to the colonizer after he has been forced militarily, or otherwise, into submission. And he accepts the colonizer's pejorative stereotype of himself and the colonizer's disparaging view of his history. He might even accept the colonizer's myth and seek to change the color of his skin, so to speak.

In the second stage, the colonized begins to resent his inferior economic and social status; he rejects the colonizer's myths and he counters them with his own myths. He seeks to resume contact with his pre-colonial historical continuum, and he tends to emphasize the uniqueness and superiority of his own cultural heritage. He rejects any possibility of assimilation and emphasizes his "otherness."

In the third stage, realizing the material if not spiritual inferiority of his culture, he seeks to modernize, and in the process of adopting Western technology he realizes that willy-nilly he will, or must,

[22] Ibid., p. 10. Suggestions for a stage approach to the process of maturity appear in Memmi, *L'Homme dominé*, pp. 17-20; Fanon, *The Wretched of the Earth*, pp. 198-99; Berque, *Dépossession du monde*, p. 143 fn. 27, and Maxime Rodinson in the Introduction to Laroui, *op. cit.*, pp. ix-x.

adopt certain of its values also. He rationalizes this acculturation by seeking antecedents for these "modern" values in his own past; he tends to argue that in modernizing he is, in effect, being true to values and even institutions that have already been anticipated in his own past, usually during its "golden age" before decline set in. But modernization is nevertheless, traumatic for him because he feels that his rationalization is not completely real; his confidence in his own heritage is shaken, and he fears that he is losing his cultural-rootings and is being drawn into the cultural orbit of the West.

In the fourth stage, he realizes both that modernization is not the property of the West alone, that it is a worldwide trend characterized by universality, and that it has led to a fundamental cultural transformation of the West as much as it has in the case of his own culture. He is now able to accept his own culture for what it has been and is and to try to preserve that part of it which is compatible with modernity and of value both to himself and to civilization as such. He is now able to be critical of his past and to see the good and the bad, the inspirational as well as the comic; he accepts his culture and at the same time he is open to the experiences and the values of others. He has become ecumenical in his attitudes and, ideally, he possesses a sense of identity that is culturally specific and at the same time he shares the universalistic ideal of the eighteenth-century Enlightenment, that of the citizen of the world.

This model of the process of maturing has been

fulfilled by very few from among the free and the powerful of the world, of course. It is not special pleading to ask for sympathy for those who have only recently, and often with little equipment, entered upon the stage of history as actors. But that sympathy should become indulgence is little contribution toward encouraging and helping in the process of maturing, the need for which is clearly more apparent today than it has been ever before in history. It is in this spirit that the quest of some of the peoples of the Third World to become free and self-reliant has been considered in regard to visions of history and to historiography.

In their struggle for self-determination the Arabs, Turks, the blacks of America and Africa, and the other peoples discussed in this essay have sought the aid and inspiration of Clio, the muse of history. They have done so in a variety of ways. Some as apologists have sought to resurrect a usually fanciful and idealized past period of greatness and glory—at their most extreme, these have been the utopians in reverse. Others, impatient with the heritage of a past, have rejected any such cult as illusory and reactionary—they have focused their attention on the future, on the technological and scientific developments of their nations, but few of these futurists have not, as devoted nationalists, implicitly or explicitly attempted to counter the image of their past propagated by the historians of the colonizing power. Thus we have seen how an Atatürk sanctioned, at least for tactical reasons, as fanciful a historical myth as the Sun-Language Theory.

The apologists suffer from the perils of evasiveness, the refusal to see their culture critically, and so realistically, in terms of progressive advance. The futurists, on the other hand, pay Clio insufficient tribute and in revenge she might disappoint their optimism about the relative ease of rapid moderniza tion. A synthesis of the two points of view might be seen in the position of what has been termed reconstructionalism whose proponents are perhaps the more realistic, combining a sense of reality in regard to the cultural importance of the past heritage with an openness to the future, but a future which will be their own.

The proponents of all three positions have made use of history for purposes of realizing national cohesion and encouraging pride and, through historical revisionism, attempting to liberate themselves from the paralyzing myths of the colonizer, if only through counter-myths. Inevitably the pole of attraction as well as of repulsion has been the West among whose nation-states, rooted in the Hellenic and Christian traditions, the "self-image" of modernity and universality von Grunebaum talks of was first forged. And inevitably, in most of the cases studied at least, the methods of the West, even the archaeology and historiography of Western scholars, have been employed by the colonized to enter the modern scene as subjects equal to Westerners who once treated them as objects in a Western drama. Inevitably, also, the attraction-repulsion syndrome of peoples seeking both "efficacy and authenticity" has led to strange myth-making. But these exotic productions, often the reflection of a national pathological state, are only early stages along the march to modernization and universalism as the "self-image" of the West becomes the common property of all men. In the future, ideally, Clio will take her place as only one of the muses of the human Pantheon, an object of interest, of culture, but also often amusement and, in the normal course of human affairs, will be given passing homage only.

192

BIBLIOGRAPHY

SELECTIVE BIBLIOGRAPHY

Abbas, Ferhat. *Lu Nuit coloniale*. Paris, 1962.

Abderrahim, Axclos. "La Réintegration de soi-même," in J. Berque, J. P. Charnay, eds., *De l'Impérialisme à la décolonisation*. Paris, 1965, 351-55.

Abdel-Malek, Anouar. "La Crise de l'orientalisme," *Diogène* 44: 109-44.

Abou, Sélim. *Le Bilinguisme arabe-francais au Liban: essai d'anthologie culturelle*. Paris, 1962.

Ageron, Charles-Robert. *Les Algériens musulmans et la France (1871-1919)*, 2 vols. Paris, 1968.

Anon. "Carnets athéniens: un peuple heureux." *Encounter* February-March, 1969: 97-106.

Apter, David E. *The Politics of Modernization*. Chicago, 1965.

Aron, Raymond. *Polémiques*. Paris, 1955.

el-Assal, Ibn (pseud.). "Return to Cairo." *Encounter* August, 1969: 76-86.

Atatürk, Kemal. *A Speech delivered by Mustafa Kemal Atatürk 1927*. Istanbul, Ministry of Education, 1963.

Ayache, Albert. *Le Maroc: bilan d'un colonisation*. Paris, 1956.

Barbour, Nevill. *Morocco*. New York, 1965.

Benabdellah, Abdelaziz. *Les Grands Courants de la civilisation du Maghreb*. Casablanca, 1958. Introduction by 'Alal al-Fasi.

Ben Barka, Abdelkader. *El Mehdi Ben Barka mon frère*. Paris, 1966.

Bencheneb, Saadeddine. "Quelques historiens arabes modernes de l'Algérie." *Revue Africaine* (Algiers), 1956: 475-99.

Bennabi, Malek. *Vocation de l'Islam*. Paris, 1954.

Berkes, Niyazi. "Ziya Gökalp: His Contribution to Turkish Nationalism." *The Middle East Journal* Autumn, 1954: 375-90.

Bernard, Augustin. *L'Algérie*, vol. II of G. Hanotaux and A. Martineau, *Histoire des colonies françaises et de l'expansion de la France dans le monde.* Paris, 1931.

Berque, Jacques. *Le Maghreb entre deux guerres.* Paris, 1962.

————. trans. Jean Stewart. *French North Africa: The Maghreb Between Two World Wars.* London, 1967.

————. *Déposession du monde.* Paris, 1964.

———— and Jean-Paul Charnay, eds. *De L'Impérialisme à la décolonisation.* Paris, 1965.

Black, Cyril E. *Rewriting Russian History: Soviet Interpretations of Russia's Past,* 2nd ed. New York, 1962.

————. *The Dynamics of Modernization: A Study of Comparative History.* New York, 1966.

Bowen, Catherine Drinker. *John Adams and the American Revolution.* Boston, 1951.

Braudel, Fernand. *La Méditerranée et le monde méditerranéene à l'époque de Philippe II,* 2nd ed., 2 vols. Paris, 1966.

Brown, Leon Carl. "Colonization—A Second Look." Institute of Current World Affairs (Tunis) May 23, 1961.

Campbell, John and Philip Sherrard. *Modern Greece.* London, 1968.

Camps, Gabriel. *Aux Origines de la Berbérie: monuments funéraries et rites funéraries protohistoriques.* Paris, 1961.

Chejne, Anwar G. "The Use of History by Modern Arab

Writers." *The Middle East Journal* Autumn, 1960: 382-96.

Chesneaux, Jean. "La Réanimation du passé traditionnel chez les jeunes nations d'Asie et d'Afrique," in J. Berque, J. P. Charnay, eds., *De l'Impérialisme à la décolonisation.* Paris, 1965, 301 11.

Chevalier, Dominique. "Une Iconographie des Maronites du Liban." *Revue Historique Moderne et Contemporaine* 1963: 301-308.

Clarke, John H., ed., *William Styron's Nat Turner: Ten Black Writers Respond.* Boston, 1968.

Dalkilic, Muzaffir Muhittin. *Étude sur la théorie Günes-Dil.* Istanbul, 1936.

Daoud, Zakya. "Le Maghreb attend son prophète." *Jeune Afrique* April 28-May 4, 1969: 14-19.

Dawson, Christopher. "The Relevance of European History." *History Today* September, 1956: 606-15.

Debbasch, C., *et al., Mutations culturelles et coopération au Maghreb.* Paris, 1969.

Desparmet, Joseph. "Naissance d'une histoire 'nationale' de l'Algérie." *L'Afrique Française* 1933: 387-92.

Deutsch, Karl W. *Nationalism and Social Communication: An Inquiry into the Foundations of Nationality.* New York, 1953.

Deuxième Congrès des écrivains et artistes noirs, 2 vols. *Présence Africaine*, August-November, February-May, 1959.

Diop, Cheikh Anta. *L'Unité culturelle de l'Afrique noire: domaines du patriarcat et du matriarcat dans l'antiquité classique. Présence Africaine*, 1959.

———. *Nations nègres et cultures.* Paris, 1955.

Emerit, Marcel. "L'État intellectual et moral de l'Algérie en 1830." *Revue d'Histoire Moderne et Contemporaine* April-December, 1954: 119-212.

197

Emerson, Rupert. *From Empire to Nation: The Rise to Self-Assertion of Asian and African Peoples.* Boston, 1960.

Essien-Udom, E. U. *Black Nationalism: A Search for an Identity in America.* Chicago, 1962.

Fanon, Frantz. *The Wretched of the Earth*, trans. Constance Farrington. London, 1967.

Faris, Nabih, "Lebanon, Land of Light," in J. Kritzeck and R. B. Winder, eds., *The World of Islam: Studies in Honour of Philip K. Hitti.* London, 1959, 336-50.

————. "The Arabs and their History." *The Middle East Journal* Spring, 1954: 155-62.

Farrukh, Omar A. *The Arab Genius in Science and Philosophy*, trans. John B. Hardie. Washington, D.C., 1954.

Fisher, Godfrey. *Barbary Legend, War, Trade and Piracy in North Africa.* London, 1957.

Gallagher, Charles F. "Language Rationalization and Scientific Progress," in K. H. Silvert, ed., *The Social Reality of Scientific Myth: Science and Social Change.* New York, 1969, 58-87.

Gauthier, Robert. "Naissance et mort du 'mythe kabyle.'" *Le Monde*, October 9, 1963.

Gautier, E. F. *Le Passé de l'Afrique du Nord. Les siècles obscurs.* New ed. Paris, 1957.

————. *L'Evolution de l'Algérie de 1830 à 1930.* Algiers, 1931.

Gellner, Ernest. "The Struggle for Morocco's Past." *The Middle East Journal* Winter, 1961: 79-90.

Gemayel, Pierre. *Six Thousand Years in the Service of Humanity*, trans. David Gordon. Beirut, 1955.

Geyl, Pieter. *Napoleon: For and Against.* New Haven, 1949.

Gibb, H.A.R. *Modern Trends in Islam.* Chicago, 1947.

198

————. *Mohammedism: An Historical Survey*. London, 1948.

Gordon, David C. *North Africa's French Legacy: 1954-1962*. Cambridge, Mass., 1962.

————. *The Passing of French Algeria*. London, 1966.

————. *Women of Algeria: an Essay on Change*. Cambridge, Mass., 1968.

Grimal, Henri, *La Décolonisation 1919-1963*. Paris, 1965.

von Grunebaum, G. E. "Self-Image and Approach to History," in B. Lewis, P. M. Holt, eds., *Historians of the Middle East*. London, 1962, 457-83.

Habart, Michel. *Histoire d'un parjure*. Paris, 1961.

Haim, Sylvia G. *Arab Nationalism: An Anthology*. Berkeley and Los Angeles, 1964.

Harkabi, Y. *Fedayeen Action and Arab Strategy*. Adelphi Papers 53, Institute of Strategic Studies, London, December, 1968.

Hayes, Carlton J. *France: A Nation of Patriots*. New York, 1930.

Heyd, Uriel. *Language Reform in Modern Turkey*. Jerusalem, 1954.

————. "Language Reform in Modern Turkey." *Middle Eastern Affairs* December, 1953: 402-409.

————. *Foundations of Turkish Nationalism: The Life and Teachings of Ziya Gökalp*. London and Brussels, 1950.

Hodgkin, Thomas. *Nationalism in Colonial Affairs*. London, 1956.

————. "What Future for Africa? I." *Encounter* June, 1961: 3-8.

Hourani, Albert. *Arab Thought in the Liberal Age: 1798-1939*. London, 1962.

Hourani, Albert. "Islam and the Philosophers of History." *Middle Eastern Studies* January, 1967: 206-68.

————. "General Themes: Introductory Remarks," in B. Lewis, R. Holt, eds., *Historians of the Middle East.* London, 1962, 451-56.

Hudson, Michael. *The Precarious Republic: Political Modernization in Lebanon.* New York, 1968.

Huxley, Elspeth. "What Future for Africa? II." *Encounter* June, 1961: 8-20.

Inalcik, Halil. "Some Remarks on the Study of History in Islamic Countries," *The Middle East Journal* Autumn, 1953: 451-55.

Jahn, Janheinz, and Marjerie Grene. *Muntu, An Outline of Neo-African Culture.* London, 1958.

Julien, Charles-André. *L'Algérie du Nord en marche: nationalismes musulmanes et souveraineté française.* Paris, 1953.

————. *Histoire de l'Algérie contemporaine, la conquête et les debuts de la colonisation (1827-1871),* I. Paris, 1964.

————. *Histoire de l'Afrique du Nord.* Paris, 1931.

————. With Christian Courtois and Roger Le Tourneau, *Histoire de l'Afrique du Nord: Tunisie-Algérie-Maroc.* 2 vols. Paris, 1956.

————. Introduction to Pierre Nora, *Les Français d'Algérie.* Paris, 1961.

————. "Retour à Alger." *Révolution Africaine* February 20, 1965: 20-21.

Karol, K. S. *La Chine de Mao.* Paris, 1961.

Kerim, K. *Outline of Modern Turkish Historiography.* Istanbul, 1954.

Kerr, Malcolm. *Islamic Reform: The Political and Legal Theories of Muhammad 'Abduh and Rashīd Rīda.* Berkeley and Los Angeles, 1966.

————. *The Middle East Conflict.* Foreign Policy Association, Headline Series 191, October 1968.

————. "Notes on the Background of Arab Socialist Thought." *Journal of Contemporary History* July, 1968: 145-59.

Khelifa, Laroussi. *Manuel du militant algérien,* I. (Lausanne, 1962).

Kohn, Hans, ed. *German History: Some New German Views.* London, 1954.

————. *Reflections on Modern History: The Historian and Human Responsibility.* Princeton, 1963.

———— and Wallace Sokolsky. *African Nationalism in the Twentieth Century.* Princeton, 1965.

Lacoste, Yves. *Ibn Khaldoun: naissance de l'histoire passé du tiers-monde.* Paris, 1966.

————, André Nouschi, and André Prenant. *L'Algérie, passé et present: le cadre et les étapes de la constitution de l'Algérie actuelle.* Paris, 1960.

Lacouture, Jean, and Jean Baumier. *Le Poids du tiers mond: un milliard d'hommes.* Paris, 1962.

Lahbabi, Mohamed. *Le Gouvernement marocain à l'aube du XXe siècle.* Rabat, 1958. Introduction by Mehdi Ben Barka.

Laroui, Abdallah. *L'Idéologie arabe contemporaine.* Paris, 1967.

Lelong, Michel. "III–Le Résurgissement de la culture nationale en Tunisie," in C. Debbasch, *et al.,* *Mutations culturelles et coopération au Maghreb.* Paris, 1969.

Lewis, Bernard. *The Emergence of Modern Turkey.* London, 1961.

————. "History Writing and National Revival in Turkey." *Middle Eastern Affairs* June-July, 1953: 218-27.

BIBLIOGRAPHY

Lewis, Bernard and P. M. Holt, eds. *Historians of the Middle East.* London, 1962.

Lüthy, Herbert. "L'Europe reste à décoloniser." *Preuves* May-June, 1969: 8-12.

Lynd, Staughton. "Historical Past and Existential Present," in Theodore Roszak, ed., *The Dissenting Academy.* New York, 1968, 87-101.

Malraux, André. *Antimémoires,* I. Paris, 1967.

Mazouni, Abdallah. *Culture et enseignement en Algérie et au Maghreb.* Paris, 1969.

Memmi, Albert. *The Colonizer and the Colonized,* trans. Howard Greenfeld. New York, 1965.

————. *L'Homme dominé: essais.* Paris, 1968.

Mercier, Gustave, ed. *Le Centenaire de l'Algérie: exposé d'ensemble,* 2 vols. Algiers, 1931.

Micaud, Charles A., with Leon Carl Brown and Clement Henry Moore. *Tunisia: The Politics of Modernization.* New York, 1964.

Moore, Clement Henry. *Tunisia Since Independence: The Dynamics of One-Party Government.* Berkeley and Los Angeles, 1965.

Moslem Lebanon Today. Beirut, 1953.

Myrdal, Gunnar. *Asian Drama: An Inquiry into the Poverty of Nations.* London, 1969.

Nasser, Gamal Abdul. "The Philosophy of Revolution," trans. Richard Nolte. Institute of Current World Affairs, March 8, 1954.

Nehru, Jawaharlal. *The Discovery of India.* London, 1951.

————. *Toward Freedom: The Autobiography of Jawaharlal Nehru,* rev. ed. New York, 1941.

Nietzsche, Friedrich. *The Use and Abuse of History,* trans. Adrian Collins. Indianapolis and New York, 1957.

Ohneck, Wolfgang. *Die Französische Algerienpolitik von 1919-1939.* Cologne, 1967.

Oliver, Roland. "Exploring the History of Africa." *Encounter* March, 1963: 34-41.

Ouzegane, Amar. *Le Meilleur Combat.* Paris, 1962.

Pannikar, K. M. *Asia and Western Dominance: A Survey of the Vasco da Gama Epoch of Asian History, 1498-1945.* New York, n.d.

Paret, Roger. "Quand l'Algérie ne savait pas qu'elle était algérienne . . ." *Preuves* October, 1966: 68-79.

Petuchowski, Jakob J. *Zion Reconsidered.* New York, 1966.

Peyrouton, Marcel. *Histoire générale du Maghreb: Algérie-Maroc-Tunisie: des origines à nos jours.* Paris, 1966.

Princeton Alumni Weekly, "A Black Seminar: The Search for Identity," March 4, 1969: 8-9.

Reichard, Herbert. *Westlich von Mohammed: Geschick und Geschichte der Berber.* Cologne and Berlin, 1957.

Rodinson, Maxime. *Israël et le refus arabe: 75 ans d'histoire.* Paris, 1968.

Rouleau, Eric. "Isräel: le ghetto des vainqueurs." *Le Monde* July 2-6, 1969.

Sa'ada, Antun. *The Syrian Social Nationalist Doctrine. The Principles and Aims of the Syrian Nationalist Party.* Beirut, 1949.

Safran, Nadav. *Egypt in Search of a Community: An Analysis of the Intellectual and Political Evolution of Egypt, 1804-1952.* Cambridge, Mass., 1961.

Sahli, Mohamed Chérif. *Décoloniser l'histoire.* Paris, 1965.

————. *Abdelkader le chevalier de la foi.* Algiers, 1953.

Salibi, Kamal S. *The Modern History of Lebanon.* London, 1965.

———. "Islam and Syria in the Writings of Henri Lammens," in B. Lewis, P. M. Holt, eds., *Historians of the Middle East.* London, 1962, 330-42.

———. "L'Historiographie libanaise, histoire de vanité." *L'Orient* (Beirut), May 23, 1965.

Schlesinger, Arthur, Jr. "The Brothers' War." *Encounter* October, 1954: 75-79.

Sebag, Paul. *La Tunisie: essai de monographie.* Paris, 1951.

Segal, Ronald. *The Race War.* Boston, 1967.

Shafer, Boyd C. *Nationalism Myth and Reality.* New York, 1955.

Silvert, K. N. ed. *Discussion at Bellagio: The Political Alternatives of Development.* New York, 1964.

Simon, Pierre-Henri. *L'Esprit et l'histoire: essai sur la conscience historique dans la littérature du XX* siècle.* Paris, 1954.

Sithole, Nadabaningi. *African Nationalism.* Cape Town, 1959.

Smith, Wilfred Cantwell. *Islam in Modern History.* Princeton, 1957.

———. "The Historical Development in Islam of the Concept of Islam as an Historical Development," in B. Lewis, P. M. Holt, eds., *Historians of the Middle East.* London, 1962, 484-502.

Stern, Richard. "History as Instant Reply," *Encounter,* March, 1969: 51-52.

Styron, William. *The Confessions of Nat Turner.* New York, 1967.

Taleb, Ahmed. "La Décolonisation culturelle en Algérie." *Jeune Afrique* December 10-16, 1962: 26-27.

Taylor, A.J.P. *Europe: Grandeur and Decline*. London, 1967.

Terrasse, Henri. *Histoire du Maroc: des origines à l'établissement du protectorat français*. 2 vols. Casablanca, 1952.

Tey, Josephine. *The Daughter of Time*. London, 1954.

The Times Literary Supplement, "Decolonising the Islamic Past," August 8, 1968: 853.

Tlatli, Salah-Eddin. *Tunisie nouvelle: problèmes et perspectives*. Tunis, 1957.

UNRWA-UNESCO: Executive Board Reports, 1967-1969 (mimeographed).

Valéry, Paul. *Reflections on the World Today*, trans. Francis Scarfe. New York, 1958.

Wallerstein, Immanuel. *Africa: The Politics of Independence*. New York, 1961.

Wansbrough, John. "The Decolonization of North African History." *Journal of African History*, 1968 (X:4), 643-50.

Zahlan, Anthony B. "Support for Israel: A Legacy." *Middle East News Letter* (Beirut), January-February, 1969: 11-15.

Zeine, Zeine N. *Arab-Turkish Relations and the Emergence of Arab Nationalism*. Beirut, 1958.

Zurayk, Constantine K. *Nahnu wa al-Tarikh (We and History)*. Beirut, 1963.

———. *Ma'na al-Nakbah (The Meaning of the Disaster)*. Beirut, 1948. Trans., R. Bayly Winder. Beirut, 1956.

205

INDEX

INDEX

209

214

215

217